LOOK FOR THE

PURPLE

LOOK FOR THE
PURPLE

Charlene Sears - Tolbert

CITI OF BOOKS

CITIOFBOOKS, INC.
3736 Eubank NE Suite A1
Albuquerque, NM 87111-3579
www.citiofbooks.com
Hotline: 1 (877) 389-2759
Fax: 1 (505) 930-7244

Ordering Information:
Quantity Sales. Special discounts are available on quantity purchases by corporations, associations, and others. For details, contact the publisher at the address above.

Printed in the United States of America.

ISBN-13   Paperback   978-1-962366-20-5
                 eBook   978-1-962366-21-2

Library of Congress Control Number: 978-1-962366-21-2

Acknowledgements

Thank you to my gift from God, Shaka Yohance, your light continues to lead me forward; Jordan & Chase your love keeps me grounded; to Nia and Noah your presence fills me. To my dear friend Kimberly thank you for leading me to my future self where this book was planted in my soul; to the other two of the triune Roz & Sojourner thank you for the strength, love, and light of our daily communions; thank you to my mother, my father, my baby brother and all the ancestors that now guide and watch over me. It is my daily prayer to make you proud. And above all, thank you to the Great I Am that I Am, my God, my Guide, my Grace, my whatever I need you to be – ten thousand tongues wouldn't be enough to express my gratitude, therefore I offer my life in service to others as my thanks. Selah.

Table Of Contents

Chapter One

Pure, Unconditional, Real, and Perfect
Love is Everywhere (PURPLE)

What if I were to offer you a little purple pill that could transform your life by changing your negative thoughts and beliefs? The pill wouldn't change your past or erase any of your experiences, but it would change the relationship you have with your past and how you view yourself relative to your experiences. No longer a hostage of your past hurt, emotions, and limiting beliefs, you would be able to access your unlimited potential and have the freedom to live a life beyond your wildest dreams. If this pill did exist, would you take it? I think most people would because, in general people have a genuine desire to live a life beyond fear and limitations. However, many well-intentioned people lack the information to get them where they want to be.

While this magical purple pill doesn't exist, the contents of this book will provide a metaphoric purple potion that offers everything that you'd receive from taking it. It will help you reconcile your relationship with your past, and transform your fears, negative thoughts, and limiting beliefs. Ultimately, it provides information, guidance, and a pathway to emotional freedom and limitless potential.

PURPLE is an acronym: Pure, Unconditional, Real, and Perfect Love is Everywhere. PURPLE represents love, joy, and gratitude. It speaks to the truth of how valuable we are, our innate worthiness, and the unique space we occupy in the world. The primary reason we don't always see this is we aren't looking for it, or have been looking for it in the wrong places. This book will help you find the PURPLE that already exists in

> As humans, we have an extraordinary capacity for self-deception because our brains don't know the difference between real and imagined, past or present.

your life. You will begin to recognize the tangible evidence of this all around you.

As humans, we have an extraordinary capacity for self-deception because our brains don't know the difference between real and imagined, past or present. We see what we expect to see, and when we have limiting beliefs, either about ourselves, others, or the world, we expect to see evidence of these beliefs and our brains oblige. It doesn't matter if what we see is real or only appears real, it only matters that it supports our beliefs.

My friend Josh, who is a brilliant therapist and workshop facilitator, introduced me to an exercise that asks group participants to look around the room and count the number of brown items they see. After a few seconds, they are instructed to close their eyes and they are then asked, "So, how many purple items did you see?" Invariably, most participants are confused because they weren't looking for purple, they were looking for brown, so they didn't see any purple. Many of them may have been so focused on finding brown that they counted rust or tan objects as brown, but very few will remember seeing purple. When they are asked to open their eyes and take another look around the room, they quickly realize there were purple items in their field of vision, along with other colors they didn't see because they were only looking for brown. This simple exercise is a perfect demonstration of how our brains work: we often see only what we are looking for. In this book, brown represents faulty and limiting beliefs, even subconscious ones. When we expect to see confirmation and validation of those beliefs, evidence to the contrary fades into the background and we only see brown.

Although our core beliefs may be subconscious, they color the lens through which we view our world, and our lives in it. This is especially true if there is an emotional attachment to the belief.

If it is my core belief that I am not lovable, I will find evidence to support this in the people, circumstances, and situations in my life. All of these things will continue to affirm and validate my belief that I am not loveable. I will see this because, subconsciously, I will attract people and experiences that validate my belief system. Although there may be evidence throughout my life that I am lovable, I either

2

won't see it, trust it, or accept it because I believe I am unlovable. This is an example of False Evidence Appearing Real (FEAR) that keeps us stuck in a vicious cycle of limiting beliefs, poor choices, and unproductive behavior.

These faulty beliefs damage the most important relationship we have: the relationship to self. There are myriad ways limiting beliefs manifest in our relationship with self. They may show up in the way in which we treat our bodies–diets high in fats, sugar, and processed foods, not getting enough rest or exercise, poor grooming habits, using drugs or alcohol in excessive or illicit ways–or staying in toxic relationships and unfulfilling careers. Perhaps they show up in the ways we allow other people to treat us by not setting healthy boundaries or being unable to say no. Changing your limiting beliefs will change your relationship with yourself, which is what determines your relationship with the world. This is especially true within our intimate relationships. Because we attract who we are at our deepest level of belief and won't allow anyone to love us more than we love ourselves, we may push people who appear to really care about us away, and instead find ourselves attracted to individuals who may not be the best for us. I've facilitated many relationship empowerment workshops and am constantly asked the secret to a healthy relationship. My answer is simple: become healthy. The healthier we become, the healthier the people whom we attract will be.

> Changing your limiting beliefs will change your relationship with yourself, and your relationship with yourself determines your relationship with the world.

Looking for the PURPLE is about shifting our perception. It is an invitation to explore different options and new possibilities, a willingness to see joy, love, and purpose in your life where you were accustomed to seeing only brown. It is as simple as consciously making the decision to look for PURPLE in all situations and experiences. Many of my clients resist such a simple response, believing it must be something more complicated. But, after spending decades seeking truth through spiritual practices and reading hundreds of books, another decade teaching psychology to college students after earning several degrees in psychology myself, over thirty years counseling and facilitating personal development workshops for thousands of people, and spending an unknown amount of time and money on my own therapy and personal development journey, I've concluded that, with the correct information, yes, it really is that simple. The challenge in this simple approach, however, is developing the courage and commitment required to become healthy.

As humans, our brains tend to overcomplicate things. We erroneously believe that the more complicated an answer or solution is, the more believable or valuable it is. In order to dispel this, I will provide scientific facts, empirical and anecdotal data, and share my personal knowledge and experience to provide a thorough understanding of the concepts in the following chapters. I recognize that you, like many others, may have layers of faulty learning and beliefs that need dismantling, and I offer this book as a guide to making that shift in perspective.

My intentions for this book are that, by the end of it, you, reader, are able to look for the PURPLE in your everyday life; that there are life-transforming shifts in your perception; and that you are surprised and overwhelmed by the amount of PURPLE that has always been present, even in your most challenging times. Seeing the PURPLE will spark your passion, and passion is the precursor to purpose. Living in your passion and purpose will open the door to a life beyond your wildest dreams.

This book will provide information and strategies to challenge your fears and transform limiting beliefs. The tools for this cognitive restructuring are laid out clearly, empirically sound, and guaranteed to work, when applied as directed. However, this book is not a replacement for therapy. If you are currently seeing a therapist, please continue doing so (it takes more than one book to heal the traumas and dramas of our lives). Whether it be your spouse, a friend, support group, or therapist, I believe we need a compassionate witness to our pain, and I encourage you to share your insights from this book with your support person.

No matter how many books we read, healing does not happen in theory as an intellectual exercise. Healing only happens through practical application, in a supportive environment with some relational connection. All of the wounds we carry, from childhood or your adult life, occur in the context of relationships. We were wounded in relationships, and we need relationships to heal.

Our belief systems and worldview aren't immediately downloaded at birth, they are shaped by the events and circumstances in our lives. If our experiences of those events are painful or traumatic, they can cause the lens through which we see the world to mute vibrant colors. Even if what we see is not brown, if we expect to see brown, the brain will ignore other colors and perceive brown. A great example of this is the Baader-Meinhof phenomenon, commonly known as the "New Car Effect". Before purchasing a new car, you probably notice very few cars of the same make, model, or color as the one you intend to purchase. But, as soon as you drive your new car off the lot, you begin to see cars with the same make, model, or color everywhere. If you buy a black Camry, suddenly the world is filled with dark colored Toyotas. These vehicles didn't appear suddenly on the roadways when you purchased yours, they were always there. Because you had no investment or attachment to black Camrys, you weren't looking for them, so you did not see them. They, and others like them, faded into the sea of vehicles you pass every day.

This phenomenon perfectly illustrates how our brains work. We see what we are looking for, or what we expect to see, or that to which we have an attachment. We become attached to our belief system because it creates and reinforces our sense of self. If our beliefs are limiting, we subconsciously seek evidence to validate them rather than contradict them, and we will notice anything that resembles our beliefs–just as we suddenly noticed dark colored Toyotas. The human brain is egocentric and needs to be right. Whether the beliefs are true or serve your highest good does not matter. Beliefs do not require rational evidence to exist, any evidence at all, even false, will do.

The limiting beliefs we have gathered are based on emotional programming from events and experiences in our life, especially those that happen in early childhood, before the brain develops cognitive reasoning. Without correct information, we will create a narrative about what these experiences must mean. This meaning forms the basis of our belief system. Like a computer virus, this corrupted data, downloaded early in the programming process, can interfere with or affect subsequent data.

The insidiousness of this bad programming is that the false information that we perceive to be true can become our truth–not actual reality, just our subjective perception of reality. We create self-fulfilling prophecies based on what we expect to or believe will happen. An example from my own life: Because I was abandoned by my father as a little girl, I held a belief that men cannot be trusted, and that they would eventually abandon me. I projected this belief onto every man I met. It did not matter if it was true, I believed it to be true, and I was constantly looking for the evidence. I didn't even notice men with the potential to be a healthy, consistent, and loving romantic partners–I found them boring. But I did notice the men who reeked of the evidence I was searching for (even though the evidence was often wrapped in a package like my father–charming, handsome, irresistible.).

The prophecy was fulfilled because I spent years being attracted to emotionally unavailable and untrustworthy men. This choice in men, like other choices, and behaviors (e.g., life, relationship, career), not only affirmed my belief about men, but created new experiences of rejection and abandonment, which created more unresolved needs, thereby anchoring and solidifying my initial core belief, and leading to more unhealthy behaviors and choices.

This pattern continues in a vicious cycle, sometimes referred to as the cycle of re-creation (which a friend of mine jokingly refers to as "the psycho-cycle"). Our lives are subconsciously controlled by this cycle until we find correct information and make the decision to stop, get off of this hamster wheel, take a moment to breathe, and look for the PURPLE.

A computer without software is basically a shell without function, and the functions of a computer can be changed with the software. Think of your brain as the hardware–a neutral organ–and your thoughts and beliefs as the software that feeds information, which encodes the computer functions. Just as computer hardware doesn't question the information in the software and applies both good programming and dangerous malware equally, so does our brain.

The process of emotional programming starts in our early childhood, with events that overwhelm our ability to cope, and creating an emotional need. As infants (no matter how cute) we are a bundle of needs, both physical and emotional. All of these needs overwhelm an infant's ability to manage. As we develop into toddlers and young children, we continue to have emotional needs, such as safety, touch, comfort, bonding, and love. If the emotional need is not met, we subjectively perceive that we are to blame, which leads to negative decisions and limiting beliefs. Psychologically, it is safer to blame ourselves for this unmet need than to blame our caregiver, whom we are totally dependent upon. So, we decide there must be something wrong with us, then make choices and adopt behaviors based on the limiting beliefs, which, in turn, creates more adverse experiences.

The following chapters will illustrate the connection between our lived experiences and the wiring of our brains through emotional programming, which colors the lens through which we see and experience life. Good news: our brains are malleable and can be rewired. Therefore, I will provide scientifically proven methods to change limiting beliefs and transform your life.

Looking at the illustration below, can you identify an event or experience that helped to create your emotional programming? What were the unresolved needs it created? What decisions did you make, or what limiting beliefs did you adopt because of those unmet needs? What were the subsequent choices and consequences? You may gain more insight as you read this book, so I encourage you to come back to this section to review and make updates.

The following is an example of how it would look were I to complete this cycle based on my father's absence in my life:

➢ Event/Experience = Feeling abandoned by my father.

➢ Unresolved Needs/Emotion = fear, sadness, anxiousness, shame, anger, confusion.

➢ Limiting Core Beliefs = I'm not lovable, I'm not safe, I'm not enough, I can't count on anyone.

➢ Choices/Behaviors = Low expectations, accepted unacceptable behaviors from others, volatile/abusive relationships.

Cycle of Re-creation = Emotional Programming

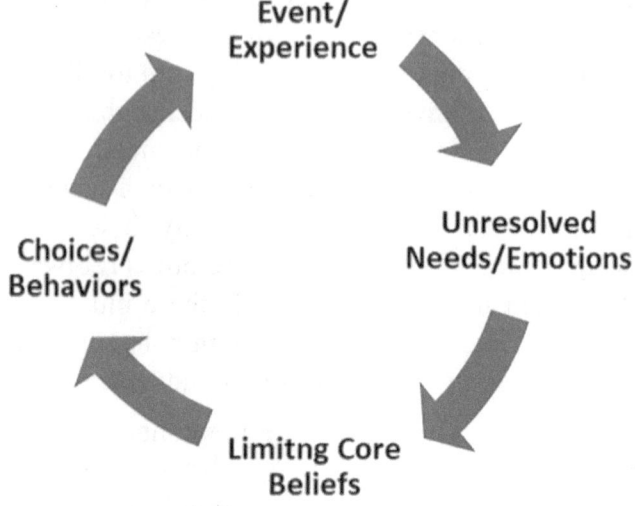

Experience/ Event	Unresolved Need Feelings/ Emotions	Decision Limiting Beliefs	Choices/ Behaviors/ Consequences

Chapter Two

What's Your Story? Just Because You Tell It, Doesn't Make It True

Let's start with an immutable truth: when you were born, you were good enough, lovable, worthy, and perfectly your perfect self. Whether or not you believe it doesn't change this truth—it's immutable. Doubt it? I challenge you to find a picture of a newborn baby (unless you're lucky enough to have a real baby on hand), look directly at the baby, and say, "You are unworthy, unlovable, not good enough, and you don't deserve good things." How did it feel saying these words to this beautiful, innocent baby? Just writing these words makes me cringe. Most of us would never say such hateful and demeaning words to a baby because we know they aren't true. Yet we subconsciously, and sometimes consciously, say these horrible–or worse–things to ourselves on a regular basis.

The truth is that we were all this baby once. We were born with an innate knowledge of our goodness, worthiness, and loveliness. But from the moment we are born, or perhaps from the time of our conception, our environment provides experiences that did not align with our truth. If, as a small child, I was called a purple giraffe, I would know this is not true because I know myself as a little girl–it wouldn't align with my truth. However, if I am told this over and over again by my caregiver or siblings, and no one provides the correct information, I would begin to take on the belief that there must be something about me that is like a purple giraffe, and I would begin to seek evidence. Maybe my skin is so dark that it looks purple (which was one of the many insults my brothers taunted me for). Maybe my legs are too long and lanky, and I have a long neck. After finding what I consider evidence, I would begin to believe that I did, indeed, look like a purple giraffe. This would affect my self-concept and create in me a faulty belief system. It wouldn't matter that this belief is far from the truth of who I am, it would be powerful, nonetheless.

Both genetics and environment–nature and nurture–color our lenses and shape our self-identity and belief systems. The good news is, contrary to previous schools of thought, the brain can be

> The old excuse of 'I'm just stuck in my ways' or 'you can't teach an old dog new tricks" has no scientific basis. Neuroscience has helped us understand the plasticity of the brain, it is malleable and can be shaped and changed throughout our entire lifetime.

reprogrammed, and belief systems can be changed. The old excuse of being stuck in your ways or that you can't teach an old dog new tricks has no scientific basis. Neuroscience has helped us understand the plasticity of the brain, that it is malleable and can be shaped and changed throughout our entire lifetime. What are the narratives and beliefs programmed in your brain? Are they true? Maybe the circumstances and experiences are true, but are your beliefs about yourself, relative to the experience, true?

We had no control over most of the adverse experiences in our childhood, yet we internalized their meanings and created false beliefs about ourselves. Both genetics (nature) and our environment (nurture) influence our emotional programming. There is a multitude of environmental, social, and familial factors and experiences we are exposed to as children–nurture–that influence our beliefs and self-concept; having a mom overwhelmed with caring for a newborn; a strained or volatile relationship between parents or caretakers; a parent's preexisting mental health issues; or other socioeconomic factors such as poverty, racism, or a lack of access to education and other resources. All of these are the circumstances and situations you were born into–but they are not *you*. Perhaps there were other events later in your childhood, such as abuse, neglect, being bullied, parents' divorce, death, or illness, alcoholism, or other addictions. These are events that happened. You experienced them, but they are not *you*.

From a genetic perspective–nature–perhaps you inherited stress/fear response genes from a parent. Scientists have proven that genetic trauma can be passed onto an individual's offspring, as well as trauma and fear responses passed energetically from the caregiver to the child. But it has also been proven that genetic predisposition and caregiver trauma responses can be reprogrammed, so, again, the excuse of *I was born this way* has been debunked.

Adverse events and experiences can trigger natural emotions such as sadness, fear, and anger, or an array of sensory responses like contracted muscles and a change in breathing. Emotions may be described as energy in motion and are as much a part of human expression as language. During infancy, when verbal skills are not yet developed, emotions and sensory responses are the only mode of self-expression and communication. Infants cry to communicate their needs, hunger, physical discomfort, or the emotional need for closeness and comfort. However, many caregivers are not appropriately responsive to their baby's only means of expression. This is not necessarily because they are not good parents, but they may be misinformed, tired, or busy dealing with their own issues. Generations of parents believed that constantly responding to their babies' cries, by holding and comforting them, would 'spoil' the baby. Attempts to quash the baby's expressions, ignore their cries, or inconsistently meeting their needs can create more confusion and attachment trauma than safety. As babies and young children without a frame of reference for rejection, or being ignored, and without developed verbal or cognitive skills to rationally process what is happening, this creates severe emotional pain.

The absence–real or perceived–of love, comfort, connection, and a sense of belonging creates a terror and suffering that can be unbearable, creating in us a disassociation, or death of consciousness. This is why we create defense mechanisms, as protections to mitigate this excruciating emotional pain. At the time we need them, these protections, also known as fear or trauma responses, are survival mechanisms.

Children have a natural self-centeredness. The world appears to revolve around them, and, in many ways, it does, within their own personal universe. We have an instinctive awareness of our value and our worth, and an innate expectation to latch onto a loving caregiver who will meet our physical and emotional needs. These are reasonable, and natural, expectations. However, when these expectations are not met, it creates a disconnect or dissonance from our truth. This truth doesn't change, we are still lovable, valuable, and worthy. However, as we seek comfort from the pain, we move away from the truth. There is a void where we expect love and care, and in this disconnect we sense the terror of not surviving. Without developed reasoning skills or language, we have no way to assess or comprehend this void, this sense of emptiness. Just as it is impossible for a newborn to walk, it is impossible for a young child to cognitively process their caregivers' issues. Without this processing ability, the child, who can only view the world from a self-centered perspective, naturally assumes that the need is unmet because something is wrong with them. This leads to emotional, psychic, and developmental distress, and begins to program the behaviors and the emotions of the child.

If an infant or young child feels threatened and doesn't receive the necessary comfort from their caregiver, or if the caregiver is the one responsible for their discomfort, an extreme psychological conflict is created because the child must straddle needing the caregiver and the caregiver being the primary threat. When we don't get our very valid needs met it creates attachment trauma. Attachment trauma is a response to adverse experiences, or unresolved conflict, in early childhood. It is a defense mechanism, a protective behavior that creates an avoidant or anxious attachment style which manifests in our adult relationships. With an avoidant attachment style, we learn to emotionally detach, avoid attachment altogether, and self-deny. As we develop, this plays out in our relationships by becoming extremely self-sufficient, detached, or appearing aloof. With an anxious attachment style, we become too attached to having our needs met by others, leading to anxiety, clinginess, and an over-dependency in our relationships. It is also possible to develop attachment responses that are a combination of anxious and avoidant, which manifests in adult relationships as come-here-go-away, push-and-pull dynamics. Either way, this original early childhood conflict interferes with our ability to trust that our needs will be met, and, if not properly addressed, it will create faulty, limited beliefs and attachment issues in our adult life.

It's no exaggeration to say that, for the first few years of our lives, our caregivers are gods to us. They emerge, seemingly out of nowhere, as giants and with our sustenance, and we are totally dependent upon them for our existence. When our emotional needs are not met during our pre-verbal stage, although we are unable to process it with words, everything is felt on a sensory level. Because the brain processes emotional pain the same way it does physical pain, activating the same areas and releasing the same chemicals, these feelings of conflict, rejection, abandonment, or neglect are extremely painful to us. We, as tiny humans, don't know the difference between the two. Attachment trauma also creates chronic stress in a tiny body without language or the ability to process conflict and can often create dysregulation in the body that manifests in chronic restrictions or other disassociations.

We know that, even as adults, the emotional pain from rejection, abandonment, or grief can feel as unbearable as a broken bone. It makes sense that we would do everything possible to avoid emotional pain. As a defense mechanism to feeling this excruciating pain, our brain learns to look for threats – signs that hurt, rejection, or

> ...the emotional pain from rejection, abandonment, or grief can feel as unbearable as a broken bone. It makes sense that we would do everything possible to avoid emotional pain.

abandonment is possible. Forever hyper-vigilant, the brain dutifully finds what appear to be threats and signs everywhere, activating defense mechanisms and protective behavior.

Every new opportunity and encounter hold the possibility of hurt, rejection, or abandonment, so we become hyper-vigilant at assessing our environment and our encounters looking for threats. This leads to a constant barrage of negative self-talk and limiting beliefs, such as *Why bother? It won't work, I won't be chosen, I've seen that look before, She probably thinks she is better than me, She is skinny and probably judging me for being overweight, I'm more qualified for the promotion but Ken is more charming and everyone likes him, I'm not smart enough to do that, People cannot be trusted, I am not making a fool of myself by asking.* These beliefs mostly come from early childhood before the adult brain is fully developed. But, even as adults, we continue to utilize the same parts of the brain we used in childhood because engaging our adult brain would expose the fallacy of most of these thoughts. However, our old brain is very powerful and creates automatic sensory responses with the power to override our thinking brain. This emotional programming cycle will continue for a lifetime, or until we begin to consciously challenge the faulty, limiting beliefs with the rational evidence that we are now capable of accessing with the cognitive reasoning skills of our adult brain.

An important aspect of emotional programming is that it is not just the events or circumstances in our childhood that program us in certain ways, but our subjective perception of those events and circumstances. Subjective perception is a term that is used to describe how we experience events and interpret their meanings relative to ourselves. What is the story we tell ourselves and others? What does this mean about me? Our subjective perspective is based on our core beliefs, values, knowledge base, and previous experience. This perception becomes our life's narrative and colors our view of the world. Subjective perception is the reason two people can experience the exact event or circumstance and have two different narratives. This is often seen starkly in siblings growing up in the same household, but who have totally different narratives about the events of their childhood.

A Course in Miracles states, "Perception is a mirror, not a fact." (A Course in Miracles, Lesson 304) We see what we expect to see. At times, our perception of the event, or the way we experience an event, may create more trauma than the event itself. The subjective perception of our lives has more of an impact on our wellbeing than our objective experiences. Here's an example from my own life to illustrate this point.

Around age four or five, I was sexually violated. Sexual abuse is one of the worst traumas a child can experience, and this was a horrifically traumatic experience for me. I was terrified, confused, and without the cognitive ability to understand or process what was happening. I cried and begged for help, only to have a dirty hand placed roughly over my mouth, ordering me to be quiet. I was told no one would help me. I was warned not to tell anyone, and that no one would believe me even if I did tell. I was terrified. Most people are familiar with fight, flight, or freeze fear responses, and I go into greater detail about them in later chapters, but, as a fear response, I was too little to fight against the perpetrator, and, being held down, I was unable to take flight and run, my fear response was to freeze. As a fear response, freezing is the least protective. Animals and humans take on this response only when fighting or fleeing is not a viable option, in the hopes of not being seen as a threat or as prey. It is the psychological hope for invisibility or safety. I wanted to disappear from the trauma, and my little body literally froze–the muscles in my neck, shoulders, and back turned to stone. Thinking I was going to die, I held my breath and entered the dark nothingness I thought was death. But I didn't die. I came out of that dark nothingness feeling bad, dirty, and ashamed. It would be decades before I took another deep breath and completely exhaled.

This was the event, and my experience of it was extremely traumatic. It overwhelmed my emotional and physical ability to cope. My greatest emotional needs at that time were for safety, love, and validation that I was good, and this horrible thing that happened was not my fault. If this event occurred and I had parents I could trust, whom I knew loved and supported me and would keep me safe, I would have gone directly to my parents and told them what happened. In this scenario, they would have reassured me that it was not my fault. They would have done everything in their power to let me know I was loved and that I was safe. They would have assured me that I was good and did nothing to deserve what happened. They would explain to me that what the perpetrator did was bad and wrong, but that it did not mean that I was bad or wrong. They would have made sure this person experienced consequence for his horrific behavior, for hurting their little girl. They would have comforted me, honored my feelings, and gotten me the professional help and support I needed to address this trauma.

If I trusted my parents to love and support me, I would have learned from this horrific event, that although a bad thing happened to me, it did not mean I was a bad person. This traumatic experience would have shown me how much I was loved, and my core beliefs would align with how important, valuable, and worthy I felt. My emotional needs would continue to be met, and while I wouldn't escape the pain or trauma, my innate sense of worthiness wouldn't be annihilated by this experience, and I probably wouldn't suffer from post-traumatic stress disorder (commonly known as PTSD, post-traumatic stress disorder is the intrusion of past trauma into one's present, causing an individual to perceive threats where there is little or no danger). In other words, the lens in which I viewed the world wouldn't have been hijacked by dull browns & gritty grays. I wish I could say that little girl grew up to be a princess, married a prince, and lived happily ever after, the end. But this fantasy wasn't my story, nor is it the story for most children who are sexually violated.

Allow me to give my childhood some context. My mom was twenty-one years old when I, her fifth child, was born. She would have five more children by the time she was twenty-eight. My birth was evidence of an extramarital affair my mom was having with my father, who was also married to someone else. My mother's husband, the father of her first four children, left after my birth, because his suspicions were confirmed by my looking like my father.

My mother was a Black woman in the American south, born in the late thirties, who had her first child at age sixteen and who, despite having separated from her husband, continued to get pregnant year after year as a single mother. While very intelligent, she had no formal education beyond high school, and she worked two, sometimes three, menial and laborious jobs to feed her children and keep a roof over our head, even if it was a very leaky roof. During orange season, she would often take all of us children with her to work on weekends, alongside the migrant workers in Central Florida's orange groves. She was paid based on the number of boxes we filled with oranges, so as soon as we could walk and follow directions, we were considered old enough to pick up the oranges that the older kids shook out of the tree and put them in the box. No matter how hard she worked, we lived hand-to-mouth in abject poverty for most of my early childhood. My mother was often frustrated, angry, and as I would learn later, suffering from undiagnosed clinical depression; she did not have the time or capacity to pamper, to coddle, or to build our self-esteem.

Because of her obsessive love and venomous hatred for my father, I was often the recipient of her volatile emotions. My three older brothers blamed me for their father leaving, and tortured me because I looked like my father, whom they hated with passion. Between my brothers and my mother, I was verbally, physically, and emotionally abused daily. Anger is often a secondary emotion that masks vulnerable primary emotions such as hurt, shame, fear, and disappointment. Because no one in my family expressed these primary emotions, anger was the emotion of choice.

I felt unloved, unwanted, and unsafe by the age of four. There was no refuge in my home environment of complex trauma; no warm, cozy place to land. Even by this early age, it was my core belief that I was bad and that my presence caused problems. My father was busy populating the little town we lived in with his seed, so I rarely saw him. As evidenced by the birth of other children with different women, my mother wasn't the only woman he was having extramarital affairs with. He once told me, proudly, that he had thirty children. Since I have only met seven other siblings on my father's side (all from different women, except for my youngest sister when he circled back and impregnated my mother again) I do not know if this is true. But I did not feel loved, wanted, or supported by him either. So, when I experienced the sexual trauma, I didn't dare tell my mother or my father, or anyone else for that matter, about what had happened to me. I honestly believed I would be punished, blamed, called bad names, and even killed because I believed it must have been my fault somehow, and that no one would protect me.

So, I didn't tell anyone. Nor did I tell anyone when it happened again, by a different family member, nor the time after that. I didn't fight or cry anymore either. I accepted inappropriate touching and sexual violation as another part of my life, and just held my breath until it was over. I internalized the trauma, and it became my dirty little secret, a shame that manifested into self-loathing and a deeply ingrained belief system of not being lovable, worthy, good enough, or safe. Childhood trauma changes our nervous system, literally causing brain damage and corrupting our memory in a way that is comparable to installing a virus on a computer. As a form of psychic protection, I lost access to many memories for decades as I separated myself from the little girl I was. I needed to be big, and, in many ways, my childhood ended at four years old. I forgot how to exhale, and it would be nearly half a century of deep body energy work before I could automatically take deep breaths, and the muscles in my neck, shoulders, and upper back began to soften.

Here we started with the same event, but two different ways of experiencing it, which led to two totally different narratives and belief systems based on whether or not the emotional need was met. In both scenarios, the event created a need for safety, love, security, comfort, and positive validation. In the first scenario–the fantasy–caregivers met the need with love and compassion, changing the trajectory of the traumatic effect on core beliefs. In the second scenario, the need was not met, which set a trajectory of complex post-traumatic stress disorder and a faulty, limiting belief system. I recognize that the experience of childhood sexual violation is the most extreme form of trauma for a child. However, your experiences don't have to be something as traumatic as childhood sexual abuse to shape your belief system. Trauma is subjective. If your experience *felt* traumatic, then it *was* traumatic.

Sometimes we may not remember where a limiting belief came from. It could have been something as innocuous as falling off your bicycle and crying because you scraped your knee, and your dad may have told you *Man up, big boys don't cry, or to stop acting like a girl.* His intent was probably harmless, but you may have developed this narrative that "real men" don't show emotions. You may feel it isn't safe or appropriate to share your emotions, so you bottle them, but we are naturally emotional beings, and emotions will find expression, in either healthy or myriad unhealthy ways. Think about the people you know, publicly and privately, that are angry, domineering, controlling, or downright abusive. I guarantee they all experienced their *version of man up* in childhood.

We all have our subjective perception. This is the story we tell ourselves, the colors that dominate our worldview and view of ourselves and others. This narrative is based on something that happened to you – it is not the truth of who you are. This sentiment bears repeating, and I will do so, often, throughout this book.

My story is not meant as an indictment against my parents, or any parent, for that matter. Today, I truly understand that all parents are

18

humanly flawed and doing their best with the (mis)information, skills, and level of consciousness they have at that time.

Most parents try their best, but we all fall short, make mistakes, and act out of our own dysfunctional upbringing, and our fear and trauma responses. We often forget that our parents are human, and, just as they appeared to be gods in our infancy and early childhood, we continue to place this god-like expectation on their ability to parent us, then personalize their inability to do so as though we are at fault. Granted, some parents just don't have the ability to parent, and some try harder than others. But I don't think most parents hold their newborn baby close to them and whisper to them, "I am going to ignore your emotional needs and mess you up for life. Oh, and by the way, I will be cold, angry, and aloof. Good luck with surviving your childhood."

> We often forget that our parents are human, and we place this god-like expectation on their ability to parent us, and then we personalize their inability to do so as though we are at fault.

None of us escape our childhoods unscathed, and no matter how good we are as a parent, neither will our children. I thought that, as a therapist, I would be the best mother in the world. My son was a miracle baby, but despite my best intentions, he did not escape his childhood unscathed. I refer to my son as a miracle because I spent my entire twenties trying to get pregnant. I loved children and I desperately wanted someone to love me unconditionally, and I thought a baby would fill that void. I felt I would be a great mother because I would be different from my mother. I would protect and love my child.

However, I couldn't get pregnant and thought I never would be because, at age fourteen, my reproductive organs were damaged when I lost my virginity during a brutal rape by some neighborhood boys. I blamed myself for the rape because I liked one of the boys and I wanted to be his girlfriend, so I followed him into an abandoned house where his friends followed and proceeded to gang rape me. It was a terrorizing and violent rape, and the next day two of the boys were playing basketball with my brothers as though nothing had happened. I was so ashamed, and my shame kept me from telling anyone. Again, my belief system was already deeply engrained. No one would believe me and besides, no one would care.

When the pain started in my stomach, I was afraid to tell my mother about it because she would know something had happened. I felt she would accuse me of having sex and being nasty, and she wouldn't believe I was raped. It wasn't until I was immobilized with pain and burning with fever that I was taken to the emergency room. I had a severe pelvic inflammatory disease, the result of sexually transmitted bacteria, and was hospitalized for over a week. However, no one, not my mother, not even the doctor, questioned me about my sexual activity. At the time, I was grateful no one asked, but in hindsight, I guess they all assumed the worst about me. Because it went untreated for so long, the pelvic inflammatory disease left my uterus and fallopian tubes scarred, and my ovaries potentially barren. I was told I would probably never be able to have children.

However, when I was nearing my mid-thirties, my son, my miraculous son, Shaka Yohance, was born and I was ecstatic. I loved Shaka at a capacity I never knew existed, and I knew I was going to be the best mother the world had ever seen. After all, I reasoned, I was now educated and had skills, knowledge, and a level of consciousness that my mother did not have as a young woman. This confidence and zeal lasted until I brought him home from the hospital, where I was so overwhelmed with the enormity of raising a real-life human that I broke down and cried. But I was determined to do better, to give him the love, comfort, and validation I hadn't received. I was determined to raise my son trauma-free, and, in my ignorance and arrogance, I believed this an attainable goal. Ultimately, I missed the mark–a lot.

I was hyper-focused on keeping my son safe from sexual, physical, and verbal abuse, my limited understanding of trauma at the time. Like generations before me, I thought I would be a better parent than my parents were because of what I wouldn't do. While this is noble and well-intentioned, the problem with this posture is that simply not doing something doesn't create a shift, it is what we do that creates the shift.

I did my best with my level of consciousness. I loved being a mom and showering my son with love and affirmation. I was the soccer mom, basketball mom, classroom mom, and all-around Shaka's Mom. I would make sure that my son would know he was valuable, worthy, and loved. I would be the perfect mom, and as most mothers do, I set an impossible goal for myself. In hindsight, it is now crystal clear to me how, as parents, we do all we can, only to have our children grow up

> Simply *not* doing something doesn't create a shift, it is what we do that creates the shift.

and recall traumatic experiences about their childhood that we were oblivious to because we were busy baking brownies.

My son had several traumatic experiences that I either missed or did not give the deserved attention. One example; when he was around five years old, I became extremely ill and was diagnosed with a rare bone marrow disorder. At one point I was even told it was terminal. I was in and out of hospitals and, when I was home, I was bedridden at times with various tubes and IVs coming out of my body, nurses in and out of our home almost daily, but I always had a smile for Shaka, the light of my life. I was married at the time, and had a large, supportive family. In my mind, my son was well-loved, supported, and cared for. He was an only child, but had plenty of cousins to play with, and all his needs were met. Within a few years, I had a clean bill of health and life went on. (Well, there was the divorce, and other issues that traumatized him, but one story at a time.)

Not until years later, when he was in graduate school, that I realized the hard truth. I learned my son lived in terror during his childhood every time I as much as sneezed. A lot of the anxiety he had as an adult was developed during those times when he lived in fear, terrified that his mommy was dying. He saw me lying in bed, hooked to tubes, with my eyes closed writhing in pain. He saw and heard things I thought I was keeping from him. My son has always been very observant and perceptive, and, even at age five, he grasped the seriousness of my health and he felt afraid and powerless, even though everyone around him would put on a happy face for Shaka. However, he was astute enough at five years old to not want to upset me, so he hid his fear from me. When he was eight, and my ex-husband (his stepfather) and I split up, I immediately got him into counseling to help mitigate that trauma. I recognized the adverse experience caused by the divorce, but I missed the trauma he experienced because of my illness.

It seems obvious now that, of course, it affected him. But, despite my best intentions, I didn't grasp at the time that my son had emotional needs that went unmet. He compensated by being hyper-vigilant about my well-being and being extra "good" so as not to create any stress for me. My son is a great man and a beautiful human being. He grew up feeling loved, valued, and supported, which helped to temper his traumas and strengthen his core sense of self, but he did not grow up unscathed. None of us do. He is a brilliant artist, and now jokes that his childhood trauma gives him fodder for his work. He has been able to express thoughts, experiences, and emotions creatively through art and music, which has provoked deep, meaningful conversations and healing for us both.

It is important to understand that it doesn't have to be a huge traumatic event to negatively shape a core belief and cloud the colors you see. Trauma is subjective. What matters is *your* subjective perception and how you define yourself based on what you believe to be true. These experiences may get buried deep in our subconscious, yet even buried, they are powerful enough to shape our belief system and color the lens through which we view ourselves, others, and the world in general.

It doesn't matter if the information we receive is false or misleading; if we believe it, we will seek, and find, evidence that proves and reinforces the belief system. Just as, in the new car phenomenon, there is an attachment to the new car that results in seeing it everywhere. There is an attachment to the belief system, and the brain, masterfully, sees what it wants to see; dull grays and browns, while all of the other beautiful colors fade into the background.

Our core beliefs, and the lens through which we view the world, are determined by how well we had our needs met as children. When there are gaps between what is needed and what is received, a child's brain can't process what is happening. These needs are natural. Not having them met is not. There is a natural order which includes the drive for survival, and as children, we are dependent upon our caregivers for meeting our needs for survival.

The seed needs water, air, and sunlight in a natural balance to become a thriving plant. The seed doesn't need higher cognitive reasoning skills to push towards the light, this is an innate behavior, an automatic survival mechanism. However, should the light ignore or reject the seed and withhold its light, the natural order is interrupted, and the seed won't thrive. Just as the plant needs light, most social animals, human included, need bonding, connecting, and emotional comfort for survival as much as food.

During the late eighties, at the height of the AIDS epidemic, so many babies were born with AIDS that entire hospital wards were dedicated to caring for them. Some volunteers in these wards just sat and held the babies, as healthcare workers found this was as important as the other medical care being provided. They found that when these babies were not held, comforted, or provided with emotional connections, they experienced emotional deprivation attachment trauma which could cause the infant to suffer from Failure to Thrive. Babies suffering from Failure to Thrive will disassociate from their bodies, stop taking in sufficient caloric and nutritional intake, and can eventually die. Failure to Thrive is not limited to critically ill babies. Otherwise perfectly healthy babies may experience Failure to Thrive if their emotional need for connection and comfort are neglected and severe attachment trauma develops.

Within the limited reasoning ability of a child's brain, if these natural needs are not met, the default rationale is that something is wrong with me. Our caregivers, with their godlike qualities, cannot be at fault because we rely on them for our very existence. Without language, this rejection and abandonment is felt on a sensory level. As we develop language, the sensory memory translates into language with plausible reasoning such as *I must have done something wrong, I am not lovable, or I am not good enough*. These thoughts and feelings form the basis of our self-concept, and this is the beginning of shame-based false evidence appearing real, which I will expand on in later chapters. Shame is a result of thinking or feeling that something is wrong with you, in response to an event or circumstance.

This shame, along with faulty information, becomes our frame of reference, our belief system. It is what we believe to be true, and what we learn to expect, or not expect, from others. Not only do we believe it to be true, but we will also defend this belief vehemently whenever it is challenged. This is why the maxim *No one will ever be able to love us, more than we love ourselves* rings with such profound truth. We will reject attempts to be fully loved with the attitude that *this is too good to be true, it is just a matter of time before the shoe drops, I'm going to get hurt, the world is not safe, or questioning what do they want from me?* and other things we tell ourselves. I've counseled individuals in what appear to be decades-long, loving marriages, but with hidden parts of themselves that they do not share with their partner because they believe it would make them unlovable. *If she really knew me, if he knew what happened to me, he wouldn't love me.* Those parts that we withhold are relegated to dark corners of secret shame, becoming self-fulfilling prophecies. We never feel completely loved because if we are unwilling to share ourselves fully, we cannot be fully loved.

As children, our emotional needs are reasonable, and ideally, they should be met. However, when they are not, the sense of rejection we feel is as painful as any physical pain. While our still-developing brain may not be able to narratively process not being lovable, worthy, or good enough, we feel emotional pain, and this sense of rejection overwhelms a child's capacity to process.

The pain of rejection and abandonment feels like we are dying because it is a form of death; death to a child's fragile sense of self, which is dependent on the behaviors of others. The younger we are, the more malleable our neural pathways and brain structures are; therefore, the shame and fear we feel imprints on our brain more. Repeated thoughts and behaviors create new neural pathways in the brain. As the saying goes, neurons that fire together wire together. This emotional programming is demonstrated in all of our relationships and comes along with us into adulthood where we rarely, if ever, question the limiting core beliefs that guide our lives.

> The pain of rejection and abandonment feels like we are dying because it is a form of death; death to a child's fragile sense of self, which is dependent on the behaviors of others.

As a little girl, I was constantly assaulted, verbally and physically, by my older brothers. They called me names like ugly, nasty, and stupid. They made fun of my dark skin, my kinky hair, my chronically chapped lips, and other things I could do nothing about. They pushed, shoved, and hit me. They practiced wrestling moves on me against my will, putting me in choke holds while I begged for mercy until I passed out. At the time, I did not have the developed cognitive reasoning abilities to process the fact that my brothers were dealing with their own trauma; their father was gone, and in their minds, my father and I were to blame. Hurt people hurt people, and they were angry, hurt, and afraid. Because they couldn't directly attack their father, or my father, I caught the brunt of their unprocessed pain.

In my childhood brain, without developed reasoning abilities, there were only two ways to interpret their behavior; they were either right or wrong–plain and simple. In my mind, there was no way all of them could be wrong, so that meant they were right. I believed I was ugly and stupid, and that everything they said about me was true. I believed I was ugly, and stupid and that everything they said about me was true.

Trauma can be defined as any experience that overwhelms our current ability to cope. The verbal and physical abuse I experienced at the hands of my brothers overwhelmed my ability to cope. It hurt deeply and I felt shame at their rejection, but they had to be right. To think they were wrong would have overwhelmed my cognitive ability to process. If they were wrong, why would they say the same things over and over? Why would they *all* think the same thing and feel the same way about me? Why did they hit me? They didn't hit our other sisters. Why didn't my mother stop them? Why did she say such mean things to me? That I was stupid, lazy, too loud, and she hated my hair, and that I looked too much like my father. I thought my father must have known those things about me, too, because he rarely came around.

Their rejection created in me a panicked fear of obsoleteness that was akin to death. This is because not being seen by those we rely on to form our self-identity is the same as not existing at all, which is a death. We need validation for our existence, and as a child, I would do anything to be seen and heard to feel alive. The anxiety in my little body manifested itself as hyperactivity, which, of course, only irritated them more, but at least they saw me.

Being ignored is just as emotionally terrorizing for adults. Think about a time when someone intentionally ignored you when you were talking or did not answer your calls or return your text. You can probably still feel the anxiety from that experience, even if it was years ago. Most news reports of domestic violence ending in murder happen after one partner refuses to talk, or otherwise engage with the other.

Who are you without your story? Who could you become without the narrative of your life weighing you down? These questions are not intended to minimize your experiences. I recognize that we have been hurt, abused, and traumatized. However, unless we can time travel, we cannot change the past. History is solid, and there is no changing our past. We can, however, heal the way our past experiences show up and limit us in the present. Pain is an inevitable part of life, but suffering is optional. Holding onto the pain of the past and making it our present narrative only increases suffering. Letting go of our attachment to the narrative frees us to transform our story from limiting to limitless.

For decades, my narrative focused on the abuse, trauma, and pain I experienced in my childhood. In many ways, I became my trauma, presenting it to the world as a badge of honor. *Look what I have been through, how much I have suffered* was my excuse for every failure and disappointment, and especially for self-destructive behavior. I rarely looked at or shared about the good things in my childhood. I thought this would invalidate my story of pain and trauma. But not until I became willing to look for the PURPLE in my childhood was I able to heal the pain.

I often ask clients to tell me what was good about their childhoods and watch as confusion crosses their faces. I have had clients angered by the suggestion that their childhood couldn't have been all bad. This is because we become deeply invested in the pain, and the story of the pain, to define who we are. However, we wouldn't have survived some of the traumatic events in childhood without some PURPLE sprinkled here and there. In psychology, these are referred to as resiliency factors. These factors help mitigate adverse experiences;

maybe a kind teacher, a best friend, beloved pet, sports, or art helped to provide an anchor, the support, or the joy we needed to survive our childhood. And, make no mistake about it, you wouldn't be here right now, reading this book, had you not survived.

There is a story about a ship caught in a storm, wrecked and torn to pieces. The passengers are tossed into the sea, holding on to broken pieces. Many are taken under by the powerful and crushing waves. Those who survived eventually made it to shore, holding onto the broken pieces of the ship. Worn, weary, and beaten, but alive. I think of painful and traumatic childhood experiences like the storm, tearing our lives apart, and resiliency factors as the broken pieces of the ship. We survived by holding onto the broken pieces. Worn, weary, and traumatized, we survived. We made it to the shore, where the healing can now begin.

Despite all the negatives and the trauma in my childhood, there was also a lot of good. There were anchors and angels along the way, and although sometimes I floated on broken pieces, I made it to the shore. When I began to heal the trauma from my childhood, I was able to acknowledge resiliency factors such as the love I was shown by my teachers and classmates. No matter what was going on in my house, I loved going to school. It was a haven for me. I had a lot of friends, was a natural leader, outgoing, and popular. I had a heart for the underdog and was not afraid to speak up for others I felt were being wronged.

I desperately craved attention, so I became a class clown, but was always at the top of my class academically. My humor was a resiliency factor, and I loved making people laugh, which, at times, resulted in disruptive behavior. But, because of my high grades, I got a lot of behavioral passes from teachers and principals. I did have behavior problems at school, but there were a lot of fun times. I talked a lot, and I had a hard time sitting still, and it wasn't until well into adulthood that I learned I had attention deficit disorder, and that it, along with an above-average intelligence, was a recipe for behavioral problems in a classroom where everyone is taught the same. Back then we did not have that language, but I am now able to understand that I was not a bad child, my energy was just poorly channeled.

When I really started focusing on the PURPLE, I remembered all the parties and celebrations that took place at our house. My mother loved all holidays and went all-out with decorations and celebration. There were always special dinners, birthday parties, and big family gatherings with my huge extended family. Because I had so many siblings, our home was often the hangout for neighborhood children of all ages. I had a constant allyship and support from my younger sister, Gwen, and knew that her love for me was unquestionable. In the time I grew up in, it was safe to roam the neighborhood and play in the woods, and so I roamed and played zealously. I had sleepovers with friends and felt loved by my aunt and my grandmother. My mother loved music and was an avid reader, so my home was filled with books and music – two things I loved as well. I was a voracious reader, and music soothed and comforted my soul. My sisters and I would spend hours coming up with song and dance routines to the popular songs, and, on good days, my mother would dance around the living room with us. I remember her teaching me how to blow bubbles with bubble gum. I remember going to the county fair with my dad, playing hide-and-seek with my brothers, and helping my grandmother bake pies and make candy apples. My mother remarried when I was around eleven years old, and we moved into a brand-new house with new furniture. My mother had a great sense of style and bought us a lot of cute clothes. My siblings and I were amongst the best-dressed kids in the neighborhood. There were a lot of PURPLE in my childhood, but for decades, I only focused on the brown. Prior to my transformation process, I never shared these wonderful and delightful parts of my childhood because I constantly sought validation for my trauma. However, I now understand these were resiliency factors that helped me to survive the traumas of my childhood, and they deserve to be honored.

In the following exercise, identify the negative experiences you had in your childhood, or any adult experiences you felt were traumatic (browns). In the second column, identify the positive experiences or resiliency factors.

Double Dare challenge: For every negative experience, identify two positive experiences (purple). Positive experiences could include your resiliency, your strength, and your ability to survive adversity. It is okay if this is the only purple you can see right now. By the end of this book, you will be able to come back and identify a kaleidoscope of colors.

Negative Experiences/Browns	Positive Experiences/ Resiliency Factors -Purple

Chapter Three

False Evidence Appearing Real (FEAR)

Fear is one of the most dominant emotions a human can experience. More than just an emotion, it is one of the two primary principles governing our existence, the other being love. Everything (and I do mean *everything*) we think, feel, or do, is done from love or in fear. From love, all good things exist; joy, hope, faith, patience, compassion, empathy, forgiveness, integrity, justice, generosity (and, of course, the color purple). Because of fear we have greed, hate, control, dishonesty, jealousy, insecurity, manipulation, and abuse. All personal problems, and all the problems in the world, can be traced back to fear.

Fear is cunning and insidious and will even mask itself as love at times. Feelings of obsession and needing someone so much that you feel you cannot live without them are not love, they are fear. So much of what happens in relationships are based on fear: control, possessiveness, jealousy, and manipulation are all manifestations of fear, even though we may erroneously identify them as love.

Although fear is often viewed negatively, there was a time in human evolution when fear was far more important to our survival than love. Imagine our primitive ancestors, oceanside, gazing into the eyes of their beloved during a beautiful sunset while hungry saber tooth tigers prowl nearby. The ability to feel fear in the presence of real and present danger was inherent to the survival of our human ancestors. No one had time to stop and smell the roses, and they certainly didn't have time to gather them into a bouquet and present them to loved ones. Their world was full of dangerous animals, harsh weather, and the unknown. The fear instinct allowed early humans to recognize dangerous and negative conditions, and to respond. Those that did not recognize and respond to danger didn't make it home for dinner, instead, they became dinner and their gene pool eventually died off. For our ancestors, feeling joy, love, and gratitude paled in comparison to making it back to the cave alive. Millions of years of fear, as a survival mechanism, created an automatic preset in our brains to fear and negativity, along with automatic fear and threat responses. During prehistoric times, automatic fear responses were a survival mechanism and included fight, flight, or freeze. With these responses, the dangerous environment could be assessed, and quicker than you could yell "lion." the fear response that would most likely lead to survival happened without a cognitive thought process.

In modern society, those fear responses are still deeply ingrained in our brain as primary defense mechanisms, and, for most of us, in the absence of real and present danger, these responses are overactive. We are mostly responding to emotional triggers with fight, flight, or freeze, and over time, we have few more, like fawn, to our toolkit. Fawn is a fear response used by modern humans as a form of protection from painful emotions. It often shows up as caregiving. Table #1 is a brief overview of our modern-day fear responses.

Emotional Fear Response Examples

Fight	Flight
Defensive Confrontational Controlling Intimidating Aggressive Bullying Critical Abusive	Addictions Avoids confrontation Irresponsible Workaholic Anxiety Manipulation Overwhelmed
Freeze	**Fawn**
Passivity Isolates Withdrawn Avoids Attention Depression Addictions Plays Small Self-Denigration	Rescuer Caretaker Enabler Self-Righteous Co-dependent Martyr Self-deny

At some point in our life, the fear responses may have been in response to real emotional threats (real and present danger), and they were defense mechanisms that protected us from further emotional harm, dysfunction, or trauma of our early life. Most of us have a primary fear response, one that we default to over the others. Which one of these is your go-to? How did you react when you sensed or believed there was an emotional threat?

- Freeze- You became small and invisible, which may have protected you from further emotional harm.

- Fight – You became aggressive or defiant as a form of protection.

- Flight – You avoided your perpetrator or your home as much as possible.

- Fawn – You tried to anticipate and meet the person's needs.

Whatever your fear response, or combination of responses, it made sense at the time as an adaptive form of survival behavior.

These fear responses only become problematic when we expect threats in all situations, seeing threats where they do not exist, and when we use our adaptive behaviors as fear responses for false evidence appearing real. What was once a brilliantly designed protection to keep us from harm can become our own self-made prison. Instead of just protecting us from real threats the fear response(s), believing false evidence to be real, begin to separate us from others, preventing the true closeness and vulnerability that is integral to developing relationships.

Most modern-day human fears are irrational and based on False Evidence Appearing Real (FEAR). I have a fear of falling, and in a high-rise building, I cannot stand next to the window because I literally feel the sensation of falling, and it terrifies me. I feel this same sensation when I drive over a high bridge. This is an irrational fear, but a fear nonetheless, and my knowing it is irrational doesn't stop the fear. Only when I began to think rationally and engage the executive cognitive reasoning functions of my brain to logically process the possibility of me falling through an unopened window am I able to soothe my nervous system. Most phobias are easy to identify as irrational fears. But what about the fear of rejection? What about the fear of being abandoned, hurt, or judged? Often, those fears are as irrational as the fear of falling through a closed window. Just as our ancestors had automatic fear responses to real, present danger, we have automatic fear responses to FEAR.

With advances in neuroscience, researchers have scientifically proven that the experiences we have, especially traumatic ones experienced during the brain's most formative years, color the lens through which we see the world. As a survival mechanism, our brains are more likely to remember the negative and adverse experiences than the good. As was just explained, remembering and being able to respond to negative experiences was necessary to the survival of the human species. Limiting core beliefs are based on FEAR. Understanding how our brains have evolved over millions of years is important to understanding our built-in fear responses and faulty beliefs. The neurobiology, physiology, and psychology of our brain helps to explain FEAR. The brain is a complicated system, often referred to as the "triune brain" because of its three distinct sections: the brain stem, the mid brain, and the frontal brain. The following descriptions are a simplified overview of our brains as they relate to fear.

The Hind Brain/Brain Stem: At the beginning of human evolution this was the only developed part of our brain. It is sometimes referred to as the reptilian brain or the primitive brain because, like the dinosaurs and other prehistoric animals, it was all we needed to survive. The hind brain controls automatic body functions like swallowing, digestion, and breathing, and other basic instincts related primarily to survival; hunger, thirst, safety, temperature regulation, and sexual drive. Like other animals, we need to eat, drink, sleep, and make babies. Millions of years ago, there was inherent danger in all these activities and the need for safety was paramount. This is where the primitive brain served its very important purpose. If we think of it over the course of life-span development, the hind brain is responsible for all the functions required for a newborn baby to survive.

The primitive hind brain is responsible for regulating emotions, fear, and aggression. Because one of its core purposes was to initiate the physiological reactions of fight, flight, or freeze in response to perceived threats, this complex structure of neurons was key to human survival. Without these self-preservation instincts, humans would have been eradicated from this planet long before any of their pre-historic predators.

Avoiding the danger of monstrous-sized predators, the perils of harsh weather conditions, and the aggression of other groups of humans consumed most of our primitive ancestor's time and energy. With an average life span of only thirty-three years, it was truly survival of the fittest, eat or be eaten, survive or die, and do it all again tomorrow. There wasn't time, space, or a need to sit around solving complex emotional problems nor was there a need for executive function decision making.

With millions of years of evolution and fine tuning of our ability to sense threats to our survival, it naturally became our genetic default setting. In modern humans, the hind brain still controls our response to strong emotions like fear and pleasure. In fact, it controls much more of our lives than many of us are aware. An unregulated response to pleasure can be just as dangerous as an unregulated response to fear. Think of addictions, pedophilia, and other high-risk behaviors were people often feel unable to control themselves.

Over time, the human brain evolved and developed many other brain structures, but the primitive brain is essentially the same, and controls the same primary survival functions it did in our ancestors millions of years ago. It doesn't reason or think, or know the difference between the past, present, or future, and it doesn't discern between real and imagined. It also tends to repeat instinctual behavior over and over again. While this is good for certain survival needs–swallowing, breathing–it doesn't serve us well when trying to change fear-based behavior. The need for survival is our most fundamental, and the primitive brain will take over our evolved thinking when it perceives a threat to survival.

Today, most threats to our survival are false or imagined, and are primarily emotional threats. Our old brain, ever vigilant, continues to constantly scan our environment to determine safety or danger, but does not differentiate between emotional and physical threats.

The Midbrain: Over millennia, as we nurtured our young and banded together in tribes for safety, the human brain began to evolve and develop what we now refer to as the midbrain, sometimes known as the mammalian brain. The mammalian brain is found in more advanced species such as apes, dolphins, elephants, dogs, and humans. The midbrain is home to the limbic system, which is primarily responsible for emotional processing, safety, social behavior, long-term memory and learning, and motivational drives such as feeding, reproduction, and relational bonding.

With the evolution of the limbic system and the amygdala, neural pathways were created between the midbrain and the old brain. Working together, the old brain and midbrain allow the development of the brain's emotional section. The emotional section is the driver of the central nervous system, and its primary function is survival. The old brain factors in long-term memories and relational bonding, via neural pathways from the midbrain, as it continues to scan the environment for threats. The hippocampus in the limbic system assesses threats by comparing present events to memories, and triggers the activation of the amygdala, which serves as the brain's fire alarm. In individuals with PTSD or poor emotional regulation, this process is often impaired or overactive.

An impaired hippocampus and amygdala results in poorly regulated threat responses and false evidence appears real. Any sight, sound, smell, or touch can trigger false alarms because they are associated with prior adverse experiences. For instance, a total stranger, with similar facial features to a neighbor that bullied you as a child could be perceived as a threat and set off this alarm in the brain. The emotional brain receives sensory data via our eyes, ears, touch, smell, etc., and, within a fraction of a second, it interprets emotional significance. If it is interpreted as danger, the brain releases stress hormones in an effort to protect us. It takes the rational brain longer to process the incoming data, and if the fear response is too intense, the frontal lobe is effectively hijacked.

If the signal sent via neurotransmitters is that there is danger, our old brain doesn't question the validity of the signal, instead, it does what millions of years of evolution has genetically designed it to do, trigger an automatic fear response of fight, flight, freeze, or, when appropriate, fawn. When an automatic fear response is triggered, the emotional brain releases hormones that activate visceral physical sensations which interfere with rational thought processes. This is the opposite of our advanced cognitive reasoning brain's ability to assess and process incoming information in a more comprehensive manner and make conclusions based on similarly processed information.

The Rational Brain/The Prefrontal Cortex:

Within the development of relational bonding, early humans banded together in groups to improve their chances of survival. This relative safety afforded more time for higher order thinking, ultimately leading to the invention of tools. Once we began to control the world around us, our brains became more centered in logic and analysis. With more sophisticated tools and processes, our brain evolved into the complex computer system it is today.

But, compared to the millions of years of human evolution, this advanced brain has only been around a short period of time–approximately 30,000 years. The thinking brain houses the cerebral cortex, responsible for higher order thinking, cognitive and reasoning functions, abstract thought, and complex problem-solving; it is the seat of the self; self-centeredness, self-identity, self-esteem, self-discipline, and all selves emanate from this part of the brain.

The neural pathways between our forebrain, midbrain, and hind brain allow us to process perceived threats with rational thoughts like, *this person is a coworker, not the neighbor that bullied me as a child.* The anterior cingulate cortex (ACC), located in the middle of the frontal lobe, is important in threat-detection. In trauma survivors, the ACC is often impaired and will determine there are threats where there are none, firing off automatic threat responses.

When affected by trauma or adverse experiences, the prefrontal cortex is not able to filter out irrelevant information and may go offline in response to fear. Within the prefrontal cortex are two areas responsible for our sense of time. When they go offline, we lose our

36

sense of time and become trapped in the moment without a sense of past, present, or future. This is why old events and experiences from the past, or fear and anxiety about the future, can feel so overwhelming in the present.

The development of the frontal lobe is also what allows us to feel empathy. There are specialized cells in our prefrontal cortex known as mirror neurons, which allow us to mirror others' movements, mannerisms, and emotional state. These mirror neurons are why, if you are happy, but spend a few minutes with a depressed person, you may start to feel sadness. We have all probably experienced being hijacked by the negative emotions of others, especially if those others are responsible for our survival, as was the case with our caregivers.

The average human thinks approximately sixty- to eighty-thousand thoughts a day. Factor in the billions of pieces of information processed every day, and we see that the complex computer that is the human brain never takes a break. It is fascinating that, with sixty-thousand daily thoughts, most people never stop to think about what they are thinking about, and because we are genetically hardwired for fear and negativity, most of the sixty- to eighty-thousand thoughts are not positive or life-affirming. Rather, most of the population spend their time rehashing the past or rehearsing the future, while missing the gift of the present. Billions of people spend days, weeks, months, and years entertaining limiting thoughts and beliefs—would have, should have, and could have—regretting the past, and making up stories about the future, without ever questioning their thought process.

Within the triune brain operates a complex system of intricate interactions and communications, forming the most sophisticated computer system known to man. This computer system relies on your input—the software—to function. Just as the brain evolved along with humankind, it evolve in much the same way over the course of one's lifetime.

At birth, the old brain is the most active of the triune brain because a newborn only has basic drives such as hunger, comfort, and safety. As the midbrain develops, we form bonds and connections to the world around us. Around age eight, the brain's executive functions such as logic and reasoning become more sophisticated, however, it is important to note that the executive functions are not fully developed until our twenties (which may help explain some of the behavior of teenagers).

Childhood trauma also has a profound effect on the development and formation of the brain. The amygdala response system is more overactive in the brains of adults who experienced trauma as children and creates faulty responses to both fear and pleasure. Developmental trauma from early childhood has been proven to affect the development of the brain, as illustrated in the graphic below.

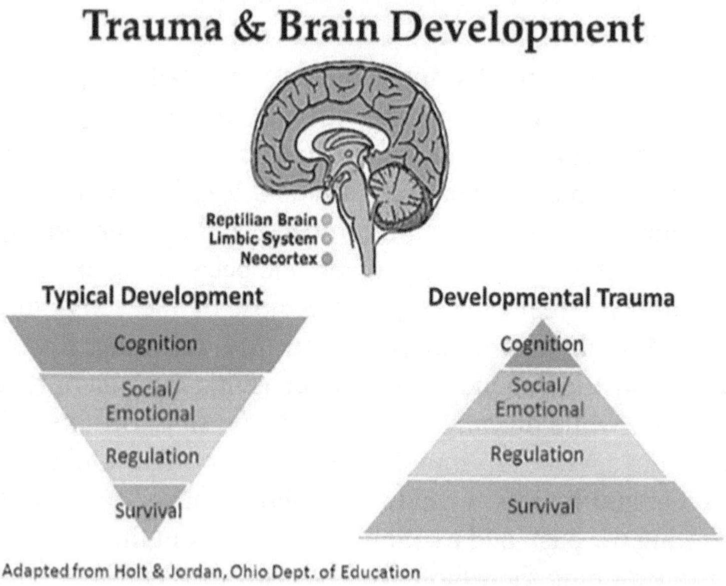

Trauma & Brain Development

Reptilian Brain
Limbic System
Neocortex

Typical Development

Cognition
Social/ Emotional
Regulation
Survival

Developmental Trauma

Cognition
Social/ Emotional
Regulation
Survival

Adapted from Holt & Jordan, Ohio Dept. of Education

As you can see in the illustration above, developmental trauma causes the brain's survival mechanisms to increase and its cognitive reasoning mechanisms to decrease. Early childhood trauma affects brain structure, cognitive development, social and emotional development, and the ability to form healthy relationships. When there has been childhood trauma, there is a heightened sense of danger, increased fear, and generalized anxiety leading to overactive defense mechanisms and fear responses, survival is the name of the game. This combination of factors can be described as complex post-traumatic stress disorder, or C-PTSD.

Complex-PTSD (C-PTSD) is different from PTSD in that there is a distortion of one's core identity, which results in significant emotional dysregulation. This usually applies to victims of chronic sexual, psychological, or physical abuse. Some views of trauma consider it a form of brain damage, much the same as a traumatic brain injury. I didn't initially align with this school of thought. However, through more research and knowledge gained, the more this explanation makes sense.

Essentially, trauma knocks the frontal lobe offline, overwhelms our brain with energy, shuts down the automatic nervous systems, and initiates an alteration of our consciousness; trauma literally changes the brain and reorganizes how we process information. After complex traumatic experiences, certain unconscious behaviors are no longer unconscious and require conscious effort or thought. For a lot of trauma survivors, me included, this manifests as an inability to breathe deeply–a normally unconscious event now requires conscious effort post-trauma.

During trauma, the ability to encode language-based memories may go offline, and the trauma is stored as sensory memory; smells, physical feelings, sounds, tastes, or sights become associated with the trauma, and, when re-experienced, even decades later, can trigger a threat response. Because the memories aren't anchored in language, the intrusion of these sensory memories bypass the frontal lobe, making them difficult to control. The old adage that says, *you can't stop a bird from flying over your head, but you can stop it from building a nest*, applies to intrusive sensory memories. You have the power to relax your automatic nervous system and engage your frontal lobe, however, because the trauma is encoded on a sensory level, it must also be addressed on a sensory level (physically, through breathing, relaxing, etc.), before it can be addressed cognitively. This is why stopping to deep breathe before responding in anger works, it allows you to soothe your nervous system and engage your frontal lobe.

Even with the development of the frontal lobe, our brain is wired such that, if there is a threat to our safety, the amygdala can override the thinking brain by using the primitive brain. From a purely biological and neurological standpoint, the overriding of the thinking brain by the old brain was a necessary survival mechanism in the face of real and present danger. Imagine one of our primitive ancestors out hunting comes upon a dangerous beast. If the primitive survival brain didn't shut down or override the thinking brain, this hunter might attempt to cognitively assess the situation. Maybe he would utilize advanced spatial and analytical skills to measure the distance between himself and the beast and combine that measurement with stored data on how fast he could run versus how fast the beast could move. If the midbrain was engaged, he might recall memories of stories heard while sitting around the fire, tales of others confronting this type of beast, and use his higher order executive thought process to calculate his chances of survival.

We can see how dangerous it can be to engage in a critical thinking process in the face of real and present danger. Humans wouldn't have survived as a species without the ability of the old brain to shut down the thinking brain in response to danger. Even now, if you were walking through the woods and came upon a snake, your old brain would hijack the rest of your brain, just as it did for your ancestors, and the second the snake is spotted, register the danger, override the frontal lobe while stimulating the automatic nervous system to send cortisone, adrenaline, and other hormones throughout the body, and react to the danger. In this second, the body's metabolism increases, and parts of the body needed for survival, such as the heart, legs, arms, and other muscles, receive bursts of fear and stress hormones and energy. There are increases in blood sugar and sensory awareness–your hearing and vision becoming hyper focused–the lungs and heart pump extra oxygen into the blood stream, sending it to the muscles. The bodily functions that are not needed–digestive functions, immune system functions, and cognitive processes–are turned down or off as the body moves into survival mode, often with nearly superhuman speed and strength, all in a matter of seconds.

Fear is a valid response to real and present danger. Healthy, life-preserving fear keeps us safe. We all need the protective survival functions of the old brain to respond to dangerous encounters. The fear we are concerned with in the context of this book is an acronym: false evidence appearing real (FEAR). Our body automatically responds to false evidence in much the same way it responds to being attacked by a wild beast. Not only is the old brain constantly on guard against perceived threats, but to validate and strengthen its position, and justify a threat response, the midbrain will remind you of all the times you were treated in an unloving manner in the past; kids at school made fun of you, your dad abandoned you, your mother called you names. Like a mosquito buzzing in your ear, the old brain will display all the alleged evidence gathered throughout your lifetime (the many shades of brown), and subjectively overlook anything else to the contrary.

If I think my co-worker is trying to undermine me in a staff meeting, I have an immediate fear response. My heart rate increases, my muscles tighten, breathing becomes shallower, and my thinking brain is shut down because I am in fight or flight mode. These automatic fear responses made a lot of sense for the survival of our ancestors, but dealing with a toxic co-worker isn't nearly the same as being chased by a hungry lion. As a matter of fact, most of us have very few experiences requiring an automatic fear response, yet they are just as active as they were in our ancestors, and we may even have dozens of them a day, each placing dangerous stress on our bodies. But, unlike our ancestors who constantly faced real and present danger, we can consciously engage our thinking brain to assess the threat.

As mentioned earlier, I have a fear of heights and falling. While attending a conference in Seattle, a co-worker suggested we have dinner at the Space Needle. Not until we arrived that I realized the restaurant was at the top of the Needle, and not only was it at the top, but the restaurant slowly rotated, offering diners a 360-degree view of Seattle. My fears of heights and falling hijacked my thinking brain and I didn't even want to get on the elevator, but my shame and embarrassment about this fear pushed me to join my colleague and other diners on the elevator. When in full fear response mode, the emotional processing of shame or embarrassment doesn't compute; therefore, it is not a factor– no one thinks about how they look or what others might be thinking of them in the midst of a dangerous situation. At this point, I still had access to my cognitive reasoning brain, and I convinced myself that I could handle going up and eating dinner. However, even the elevator was made of glass, offering views on the way up to the restaurant. My entire cognitive reasoning brain went offline, and I nearly passed out on the ride up. Shame and embarrassment were no longer concerns and I was unable to hide my increasing panic and fear. I moved to the farthest point from the glass door, turning towards the back wall. The chuckles from other passengers only exacerbated my increasing anxiety.

When we arrived at the top of the space needle and entered the restaurant, we were seated next to a window and my anxiety began to take over my nervous system. There was a visceral, physical reaction in my body, I was sweating, and my heart felt as though it could burst through my chest. As irrational as this may sound, my old brain believed I was in danger of falling through the closed window, or that the entire restaurant might topple over, sending us all crashing to our death. The only way I was able to manage this increasing terror was through a breathing technique that relaxed and soothed my sympathetic nervous system enough to access my thinking brain and examine the holes in the evidence that appeared very real to my old brain. I asked myself questions about physics like *Could I really fall out of a closed window? What are the chances that this restaurant would slide off its base and crash to the ground?* Asking and answering these questions after I had soothed my nervous system allowed me to recognize the holes in the evidence, rendering it false. Had I asked those same questions while my fear responses were overactive, my irrational old brain may have answered, *Hell yeah.* While the irrationality of this fear may be crystal clear to others, it is important to understand that this fear of falling is just as irrational as some of the emotional fears we face and requires the same mitigation process. Calm the nervous system and engage the thinking brain. A sudden request to meet with your boss or a text from a partner wanting to "talk" could trigger a fear response that hijacks the thinking brain the same as a fear of heights. Stop, breathe, exhale slowly deeply, and engage your thinking brain with logic.

Contrary to the original lifesaving purpose of fear responses, when dysregulated, these responses are dangerous, and potentially deadly, to modern humans. Fear can create excessive stress, and we all know the dangers of too much stress. Stress hormones like cortisol and adrenaline, when produced in excess, are responsible for all manners of mental and physical health problems such as heart disease, digestive issues, immune system dysregulation, cancer, anxiety, and shortened lifespan. In highly stressed people, the connection between the prefrontal cortex and the amygdala (which governs emotional regulation) begins to deteriorate, causing the amygdala to increase in size and poorly regulate emotions, because it cannot readily receive the neurons carrying logical information from the prefrontal cortex.

In recent years, groundbreaking research has provided a better understanding of trauma's effect on our health and our lifespan. The Adverse Childhood Experiences (ACE) study, one of the most well-known studies in the field, ironically, began with a focus on social determinants for poor health outcomes. However, the empirical data collected overwhelmingly found that the primary determinant to poor health outcomes was adverse childhood experiences.

In this landmark study, the Center for Disease Control (CDC) and Keiser Health conducted large-scale, long-term research on health and social determinants. By studying over 17,000 adults, mostly college educated, White, and middle-class, who were at increased risk for heart disease, obesity, autoimmune illness, cancer, depression, and addictions, they found an overwhelming correlation between these kinds of poor health outcomes and adverse experiences in childhood, with over 21% reporting childhood sexual abuse.

This study is the single-most important study on the effects of childhood trauma. As a result of this research, the CDC and Kaiser Health identified ten adverse childhood experiences (ACEs) proven to significantly affect adult health and wellbeing. Although, there could be more than ten traumatic events experienced during the first 18 years of life, the top ten were:

1. Having a parent or other adult in the household who often swore at you, humiliated you, or acted in ways that made you feel you might be physically harmed.

2. Having a parent or other adult in the household who often pushed, grabbed, slapped, threw things at you, or ever hit you hard enough to cause injury or leave marks.

3. Having an adult, or a person at least five years older than you, touch or fondle your body, or have you touch or fondle their body in a sexual way. Or having an adult, or a person at least five years older than you, attempt, or engage in oral, anal, or vaginal intercourse with you.

4. Often feeling that no one in your family cared for you, or that your family didn't look out for each other, or provide support to each other.

5. Often feeling that you did not have enough to eat, had to wear dirty clothes, and had no one to protect you. Or your parents were often too drunk or high to take care of you, or take you to the doctors, if needed.

6. Your parents were separated or divorced.

7. Your mother, stepmother, or other female caregiver was often physically abused or threatened with physical abuse or death.

8. Having lived with anyone who was a problem drinker or drug user.

9. Having a household member who was depressed or mentally ill, or having a household member attempt, or commit, suicide.

10. Having a household member who was incarcerated.

Again, there are other traumatic or adverse childhood events that could influence you as an adult, but these are the primary ten identified in the study. To identify your ACE score, add one point for each one of the adverse conditions you experienced during your childhood. An individual's ACE score is a determinant of both physical and mental health. Individuals with an ACE score of four or higher have an increased risk for suicide (1550%), heart disease (250%), and they are 700% more likely to become an alcoholic, along with a host of other chronic health and mental health issues.

While there may be significant differences between a person with an ACE score of one and a person with a score of four, research has found that once you reach an ACE score of six, the determinants flatline and there isn't any statistically significant difference between a person with a score of six and a person with a score of ten.

Understanding your ACE score can be good information to have, but what is more important to understand is that you are incredibly adaptive, and your ACE score is not an automatic life sentence. Even with an ACE score of ten, you have managed to survive, you have found this book, and you can reprogram the faulty and limiting belief system developed due to these adverse childhood experiences.

Because of adverse experiences, the brain is conditioned to respond to ordinary stress and uncomfortable emotions with the same response of early humans running away from life-threatening danger. A co-worker says something triggering and we find ourselves at work with a racing heart, sweaty palms, and tense muscles, or in traffic with road rage and adrenaline pumping through our bodies. These over reactive fear responses are the reason a simple statement by a friend or partner can trigger an outburst seemingly totally out of proportion.

One morning I was making breakfast, and my boyfriend held a waffle up to show me it was burned. Because he only held the waffle up for me to see, and didn't say anything, I did not know what he was thinking. Typically, when we sense a threat, but we don't know what someone is thinking, or exactly what the threat may be, we make up a story of what it must be. Although I wasn't out in the jungle being chased by a wild animal, I immediately felt under attack, and had an automatic fear response. I felt the same shame-based fear as when I was being called stupid by my brothers, and the same fear of rejection as when I was abandoned by my father. It was overwhelming. In just a matter of seconds I had gone from a strong, confident woman making breakfast for her man, to suddenly feeling at risk of annihilation.

Of course, I am not processing any of this in the moment, because it all happened in a spit second and my amygdala had shut my cognitive reasoning brain down. My sympathetic nervous system was sent into overdrive and my primitive reptilian brain was in control. My heart was racing, muscles tight, and my arms folded up across my chest as if to protect my internal organs–I was in fight mode, standing wide-legged in the position of a warrior. In that moment I felt my entire being was threatened. It was no longer about the waffle. Old beliefs like *I am not lovable, I am not good enough, he is making fun of me, he is rejecting me, he will abandon me*, all clouded out my reasoning ability.

My perfectionism, or the belief that I need to do everything perfectly and without room for failure or I would be punished and rejected, further increased my over-activated sympathetic nervous system. Growing up in a household where mistakes weren't tolerated, and a dish broken by accident meant a physical beating, I was terrified of the perceived punishment for burning the waffle. The sight of the burned waffle was the trigger that evoked the sensory memory. Accident or mistake, it didn't matter. I felt danger. The frontal region of my brain, the region responsible for location and time, and my thalamus, responsible for integrating the data from incoming sensations, were both shut down. In this moment, my emotional brain, which isn't under conscious control and can't communicate through words, had taken over. I began to cry, and because I was angry at myself for crying, I projected my anger at him, screaming at him that he should have made the damn waffles because I was already doing too much as it was. I saw the shocked look on his face, but because my frontal lobe was offline, it was not registering. His stating that I was overreacting made me feel invalidated, as though what I felt did not matter, and only turned my defensiveness up.

At that time in my life, I did not have knowledge or understanding of brain science and fear responses. But there I was, in my 30-year-old body, standing in the kitchen of my home, where I paid the bills with money I earned from my very adult job. Yet, from an emotional standpoint, I was five years old, and my old brain was trying to protect me from the rejection of my mean and abusive brothers or the wrath of my mother. I had a full emotional meltdown because of the burned waffles.

Only later, when my nervous system finally calmed down and I was able to access my cognitive reasoning brain, did I see the ridiculousness of my reaction. I felt bad about my behavior, and humbly apologized. We laughed about it later, and it became one of our inside jokes (but he made all the future waffles because there was still a part of me that believed I couldn't make good waffles and I would be ridiculed. I stopped making waffles for years.) I now enjoy making waffles and make them for my family and friends all the time. I know that if one burns or is undercooked, it's no big deal because I can just make more. Yes, knowledge is power, and in this case, it is also pleasure because I do love hot buttery waffles.

But at the time, my old brain had been unable to distinguish between a slightly burned waffle and my faulty core beliefs about myself, even though it was false evidence appearing real. He was rejecting the waffle, not me. But, without the ability to access my logical brain, I and the waffle were one in the same. The primitive brain lacks rational reasoning ability; therefore, it responds to all fears as a threat to our survival. Whether it be a saber-toothed tiger or rejection from our partner, the primitive brain's response is the same.

This incident (not one of my proudest moments) helps illustrate how old fears and limiting beliefs can hijack our brain and prevent it from seeing anything but brown. The folk wisdom of counting to ten before reacting in anger is an intervention technique now proven by science. If we can stop, slow our breathing, become mindful of our surroundings, and relax our bodies we are better able to engage our frontal lobe to assess the situation with reasoning. Had I been able to do this when I burned the waffle, my response might have been a simple *oops, I didn't realize it was burned, I will make you a fresh one*, end of story. But, because I was emotionally hijacked by my faulty beliefs and my thinking brain was not in control of my response, I wasn't able to do that.

Emotional hijacking happens when the amygdala's emotional response is out of proportion to the stimuli. We've all had our version of the waffle scenario, where one glance or word about something trivial hijacks our thinking brain. The brain perceives an emotional or physical threat based on our perception of memories and/or experiences, and an alarm goes off in the amygdala, shutting down the thinking brain and alerting the reptilian brain to activate the hypothalamus pituitary adrenal axis, releasing cortisol into the blood stream and triggering the fear response. With limited access to our brain's cognitive reasoning, the sympathetic nervous system is hyper aroused, and fear takes control of our unconscious body functions such as breathing, swallowing, and digestion.

While these thoughts of being unlovable or unworthy appear to be real, they are not. They are based on false evidence that we collect throughout our lifetime. We may even plant evidence by sabotaging relationships and opportunities because of our fear, or by only being attracted to individuals that will validate the faulty beliefs. This process builds and solidifies your belief system by seeking out the brown in every encounter so that even a rainbow of colors only appears as various pale and muted shades.

Just because someone treats you in an unloving manner doesn't mean you are unlovable. This so-called evidence has nothing to do with you but speaks to the behaviors of others. If your father abandoned you, if your mother was abusive, if you experienced sexual abuse, or kids making fun of you, this says more about them than it does about you. However, it can be difficult to see this without engaging the advanced cognitive reasoning abilities, and challenging the evidence provided by our mid- and old-brain. The old brain develops neural pathways based on the false information we feed it, eventually creating limiting beliefs that color the way we see the world. When we see potential threats everywhere, our survival modes are triggered.

The best way to confront fear is to confront fear. Don't hide, don't run, but turn and face the fear. Question the accuracy of the evidence because FEAR's power is in its ability to make us perceive danger even when it doesn't exist. Hiding and avoiding gives FEAR its power because, if you do not look at the threat, you will not be able to process the reality of the threat. Early in my healing journey, I had a dream, or, rather a nightmare, that changed the way I thought about fear forever.

> Fear's power is in its ability to make us perceive danger even when it doesn't exist. Hiding and avoiding gives FEAR its power because, if you do not look at the threat, you will not be able to process the reality of the threat.

In this nightmare, I was being chased by a half-human half-beast character, at least ten feet tall, with blood red eyes, covered in slimy, matted fur. Its fingernails and teeth were yellowed, a foot long and razor-sharp. I was running down an unknown street, nearly out of breath, the monster close on my heels. I ran to a dead end and had no choice but to run into a huge, old, house – the. My heart was pounding, and I was trying to yell, but as is typical in nightmares, there was no sound. The further I ran into the house, the larger it seemed to grow. I ran into one of the endless rooms but was unable to lock the door behind me. I ran through a door into a large room, only to see another door and run through that door. I was running through those doors, terrified, when I finally entered a room with no other doors. There was no way out except back the way I came, which wasn't an option because the monster was still in pursuit. I felt helpless knowing that, at any time now, I would be shredded to death. I was trapped, and ready to accept my death, praying only that it came quickly.

Suddenly, I realized the absurdity of the situation. The brief thought that this monster couldn't be real was all it took to empower me. My helplessness and resignation turned to anger, and I realized I had a choice: run and crouch in the corner waiting to be consumed by the monster or fight for my life. The second I made the decision to fight, I saw a broom in the corner of the room. I grabbed it, turned towards the monster, and swinging it wildly, I dared the monster to come closer. I felt emboldened, determined to fight for my life. Instead of running from the monster, I ran towards it. The monster shrunk backwards. Was it afraid of me? I was surprised, but also filled with courage. I charged with all my might and this larger-than-life monster shrank into a tiny mouse and scurried out of the room. I woke up soaked in sweat and out of breath, but I felt powerful. The monster of FEAR had tried to consume me, but I confronted the FEAR, and I won.

What are your fear monsters? What is so powerful and scary about them? Are they real, or just an illusion? The power of FEAR lies in the darkness it inhabits, and the shadows it casts. FEAR cannot maintain the same power in the light of examination that it does in the mind's dark recesses. Most fears are illusions, just stories we make up about what *might* happen. Turn and look at your fear. Simply acknowledging FEAR activates the executive thinking part of the brain.

In his groundbreaking book on trauma "The Body Keeps the Score", Dr. Bessel Van Der Kolk states that all trauma is pre-verbal because it drives us to the edge of comprehension, cutting us off from language based on common experience or an imaginable past. Fear does the same thing to us, cutting us off from our rational brain. Examine the FEAR. Give it a voice. What is it trying to protect you from? Is there real and present danger? If so, are you capable of handling the worst-case scenario? What happens if you do nothing? Is standing still a viable option? Ask yourself these questions and engage your cognitive reasoning brain to provide the answer.

The following is a process for managing fear that includes recognizing, understanding, cognitive processing, and action.

1. Recognize It: Remember fear has many manifestations. When we aren't being honest or are trying to control a situation, this is an expression of fear. Acknowledge it from a place of compassion, not judgement. Recognizing and acknowledging fear increases the executive order functions of the thinking brain, and interrupts the direct neural pathways to the old brain. When you recognize negative thoughts or behaviors, ask yourself, *what am I afraid of?* Bringing this awareness of fear into your conscious mind better positions you to deal with the fear. Remember that millions of years of fear-based thinking ensured the survival of our species and became our genetic default setting. Remember that our fears are developed to protect us from emotional harm, and that examining these fears is the first step in changing faulty and limiting beliefs. You will never be able to judge, or shame yourself into healing, only through compassion and love do we heal.

2. Understand It: Where does this fear come from? Most fears are based on our subjective perception of past events. The fears may have been valid at some point in our lives, but we don't have to keep reaffirming the false beliefs and re-creating those negative situations through our fears. My father was not there for me as a child. Consequently, I developed a belief system that I was not worthy of love, and my core fear was rejection and abandonment. I began to develop protections to defend myself against these fears, such as manipulation and self-compromising behaviors in order to feel loved or accepted. Understanding the basis of your fear is important and will help you have compassion for yourself.

3. Cognitive Processing: Write about the emotions, thoughts, or behaviors that your fear brings about. Write about where you feel your fears are coming from. You may speak directly to your FEAR. Remember that the old brain thinks there is a life-threatening danger. Lean into it by asking FEAR what it is trying to protect you from. This works best if you write the question down and respond with your first thoughts. Don't overthink the response.

Freeform writing can be a valuable tool in this process. This is a mindfulness writing exercise that allows you to access your subconscious thoughts. All you need is a pen or pencil, paper, and an alarm. Set the alarm for three to five minutes and write down every thought that comes to your mind, no matter how seemingly irrelevant. Always start with a sentence prompt. In this case, a helpful prompt might be something like, *I am fear, and what I am trying to protect you from is… or What I am really afraid of is…* You may have random thoughts about whether or not room temperature water really is better for you, or the fact that you really need a manicure. Write it all down without judgment.

When you are freeform writing, there is no need to try analyzing the thoughts–you can do that later. For the purpose of the exercise, the pen should never stop moving on the paper. I have facilitated this exercise hundreds of times, with thousands of individuals, and no matter what the prompt is, most are surprised by the amount of clarity and understanding they achieve from just a few minutes of this exercise.

4. Action: Just do it. The best way to confront fear is by confronting fear. Develop a plan to move through the fear. Find an accountability partner, someone who will lovingly support you as you move through your fear. Most of our fears stem from a time when we were powerless to take care of ourselves, and the old brain doesn't know the difference between now and then. Do the thing that you are afraid of; make that phone call, ask for a promotion, end the relationship. Turn towards fear and say, *I recognize you as fear, but I am moving forward. I know you are trying to protect me, but I am an adult now, and I am perfectly capable of taking care of myself.* The goal is not to be fearless. Remember that courage is not the absence of fear but the ability to move forward even when we feel afraid. There will always

be fear because it is a hardwired default setting. The primitive part of our brain likes familiarity and repetition, and there is a relative safety in the predictable. Change and the unfamiliar are seen as threats, however, change is a necessary part of growth. Change and growth only happen outside of our comfort zones, and guess what? Outside of the comfort zone is uncomfortable. Make peace with this discomfort. If you do not feel fear about something in your life, then, my dear, you are living way too small.

Use the following exercise to further examine the core of your false evidence appearing real (FEAR).

Give your responses below careful consideration to get closer to the root of your fear. For instance, if your fear is, *I am afraid I am going to lose my job*, do some unpacking to see if you can get deeper. The process may look something like this:

Q: Why are you afraid of losing your job?
A: Because I will not be able to pay my bills.

Q: Why are you afraid of not being able to pay your bills?
A: Because I will not be able to take care of myself.

Q: What do you believe it means about you if you were not able to take care of yourself?
A: That I am a failure

Q: What would happen if you were a failure?
A: I would be judged and ridiculed.

Q. What do you believe it would mean about you if you were judged and ridiculed?
A. That I am not good enough, I am not worthy.

As we drill down, we see that the surface fear is about losing the job, but the core fear is the fear of being judged and ridiculed, which is based on the limiting belief of not being good enough or worthy. Use the next exercise to further examine your core fear(s).

What are your fears?

I am afraid of…

_____

_____

Where does the fear come from? Often your fears are based on your beliefs about you or about life. It is important to understand where the fear is coming from.

This fear comes from my belief that…

_____

_____

How do you respond when you are afraid? For instance, do you become judgmental? Do you attempt to control? Do you isolate? Do you compromise?

What I do when I am afraid is:

_____

_____

How can you confront your fear(s)? Doing the opposite of what you would normally do when you are afraid is often a good way to confront your fears. (i.e., attending social functions, spending the weekend alone, speaking up in the staff meeting, etc.)

I will confront my fear by:

_____

_____

Chapter Four

You Are Who You Think You Are:
Decisions and Limiting Core Beliefs

As discussed in previous chapters, the brain is a neutral organ that responds to stimuli and input. It cannot distinguish between what is real and imagined, nor can it differentiate the past from the present or future. This lack of discrimination helps explain the power of faulty beliefs. When we affirm something to ourselves, the brain accepts the information indiscriminately, and we come to believe it. This pattern of thought becomes our emotional programming. Through repetition, thoughts and beliefs forge well-established neural pathways in the brain, transforming the process into an automatic one. Much like the daily commute to work that, once familiar, requires minimal cognitive effort, these thoughts unfold automatically. Perhaps the first few times you navigate an unfamiliar route, it requires the executive function of your brain to navigate the route, but once it becomes familiar, executive-level cognitive processes are no longer necessary. Often, we reach a destination without a clear memory of the journey because our brain is on autopilot, tuning out the details along the way. The same applies to faulty beliefs traveling well-trodden neural pathways, bypassing the thinking brain. Just as we arrive at a familiar location without consciously considering how we got there, the same is true for faulty beliefs.

Limiting beliefs are extremely powerful, no matter how false the evidence. They form our self-concept and our self-esteem. As a child, I often felt stupid because this was the favorite verbal attack in my household. I was being told that I was stupid, therefore, despite making straight A's, always being on the honor roll, and winning spelling bees, I internalized this belief and still felt stupid. My grandmother and mother had no formal education, but they were two of the most intelligent women I knew. Their intelligence gene was obviously passed along because quite a few of my siblings are highly intelligent and were academically superior. I did not feel smart in comparison to them–they were also making the honor roll–and most of my teachers, who had previously taught my older siblings, expected me to excel academically as well.

My mother appeared to take her children's intelligence for granted and didn't seem to value education in the traditional sense. However, my mother had an obvious love for books and she read all the time. Alongside our regular library trips, our home was consistently filled with books. We were the first family in our neighborhood to have the complete volume of encyclopedias, which was a big deal back in the early seventies. However, I don't recall ever receiving praise for good grades. I was a Sears and achieving high grades was simply what we did.

It was not until I was nearly thirty and started college that I began to understand I wasn't stupid, but that I had above average intelligence. There had been a ton of evidence throughout my life that pointed to my intelligence, but I still believed I was stupid. I was very insecure around people I deemed smart or educated because I thought they would see I was stupid. In fact, I was so insecure that I wouldn't talk when I was around people that I thought knew more than me.

During my late teens, I experienced an abusive relationship, and I almost developed selective mutism. Living in constant fear of abuse or ridicule, I spoke very little. I felt so inferior that around most people, it seemed as if my brain would lock and I couldn't find words that made sense, so I kept to myself, only making sounds when a response was required. Now anyone that knows me knows that I am a natural chatter box. In fact, most of my behavioral issues stemmed from my struggle to remain quiet. However, in this particular relationship, my feelings of inadequacy were so intense that I rarely spoke. That is the power of faulty beliefs.

The good news is the brain is malleable and it can be reprogrammed. Once you stop using a neural pathway by eliminating repetitious thoughts and faulty beliefs that neural pathway would begin to shrink. Just as a well-worn path through the woods begins to disappear as it is covered with vegetation when the path is no longer used, the same is true for the pathways in our brain. Therefore, since our brains are malleable why not create pathways and patterns to our best life. Positive, life-affirming repetitious thoughts and behaviors create new pathways in our brains and can become our default setting. As the spiritual writer | If you stop using a neural pathway by eliminating repetitious thoughts and faulty beliefs that neural pathway would begin to shrink. Just as a well-worn path through the woods begins to disappear as it is covered with vegetation when the path is no longer used, the same is true for the pathways in our brain.

Mike Dooley often says, "Thoughts become things, so think good ones."

Again, the old brain doesn't know the difference between the past or the present, what is real or false, or me or the waffle. It has been conditioned to respond to any stimulus it perceives as a threat with a defensive posture. Our very survival depends on being able to identify threats and respond. If your core belief is, I am not lovable, your brain will constantly scan the terrain to find the evidence of not being lovable to better position for the defense. Not because it wants to harm you, but on the contrary, it wants to protect you. Therefore, it scans the environment for threats based on memories of past hurts and rejection. It will seek and file what appears to be evidence that proves that you are not lovable. It will initiate a fear response and it will remind you of the evidence as justification for the fear response – before you are hurt. It is the old tactic of the best offense is a defense.

Growing up in a poor rural community in the Jim Crow south during the sixties, there were many cultural norms that were adopted as survival mechanisms, but they also supported my faulty beliefs of being inferior. I was born in Winter Garden, Florida which is adjacent to Ocoee, Florida, the site of the deadliest voting day massacre in America's history. In 1920, two Black men attempted to exercise their rights to vote, which led to entire Black families murdered, their homes and business burned to the ground. Those that were not murdered were chase out town by an angry white mob that grew in strength and numbers as other Whites in neighboring towns joined the massacre.

Forty years later when I was born there were still surviving victims that lived in Winter Garden, and all Black folk lived in fear of the town on the other side of the railroad tracks and the White men that lived there. Every Black person throughout Central Florida knew Ocoee was a sundown town – meaning they couldn't be caught passing through Ocoee after sundown or they would become strange fruit swinging from a tree by daybreak.

During the sixties, Central Florida's land mass was covered with orange groves. While picking oranges was laborious and hard work, it was more desirable than the cotton and tobacco fields of the antebellum south. During the same period of the great migration north by black folk seeking a better life than what was available down south, there was also a migration further south from Georgia, Alabama, and the Carolinas to sunny Florida. My grandmother was amongst those that migrated to Central Florida when my mother was six years old.

However, my childhood was not filled with palm trees and beaches. While Florida was not considered the antebellum south, the orange picking industry was very much the same as the post-slavery share cropping system. Often the houses and store in the 'quarters' were owned by the same folk that ran the orange groves and they would take their rent and any store credit owed right out of the money earned by the workers in the orange groves. Entire families (mine included) would work these groves from sunup to sundown. The adults and the bigger kids climbed the trees and picked or shook the oranges down and the smaller kids picked the oranges up off the ground and put them in the boxes.

As a little girl, I experienced the assault on my psyche of the Jim Crow racist south when I was not allowed to use a 'White Only" bathroom in downtown Winter Garden and was forced to empty my bladder behind a row of parked cars. This was in the mid-sixties, and it would not be until 1973 that Central Florida schools were forced to integrate. Even then, Ocoee did not have its first Black citizen until the early 1980's. As a little poor Black girl, the messages regarding my value and self-worth that were inherent in the racist Jim Crow system had an obvious effect on my self-worth.

When I was five, my mother gave away my older sister to a couple that wanted a little girl. We were only eleven months apart and I had spent every day of my life with her and then she was gone. This scenario repeated itself three more times by the time I was seven. My mother had six girls and she gave four of them away.

As bizarre as this may sound it was not uncommon for poor blacks to parcel out their children (a practice no doubt with origins steeped in the inhumane practices of slavery). Unfortunately, Black folk adopted many of these cultural norms as survival mechanism. In many ways for me (and I imagine countless other little Black boys and girls) this practice was more traumatizing and damaging to me than the sexual abuse. Imagine playing with your little sister one day and coming home from school the next day to find her gone, without any explanation. To make matters worse, my older brothers acted like this was normal and they got angry at me for questioning the whereabouts of my sisters. They were afraid of upsetting my mother, and they made me feel like I was the crazy one in the family. As bizarre as this sounds, they were trying to normalize this abhorrent behavior.

My mother attempted to give me away, but my grandmother came and brought me back home. But I often wished that someone would take me away from the house of horrors that was my childhood home. I wanted to feel special, to feel like I mattered to someone. I wanted to be chosen. But I would be constantly reminded by my siblings and my mother that I was too loud, too messy, talked too much, moved too much, and was generally just too much for anyone to deal with. My old brain used this alleged evidence against me for the better part of my life. This has been the most difficult belief to exorcise, and I can still get triggered by certain family members saying I am 'too dramatic' or if I am being told to 'stop talking'. However, the difference today is that I have an arsenal of contradictory evidence and I am able to consciously engage my thinking brain to process the fallacy of this belief system.

Fear-based limiting core beliefs triggers an overactive survival response that perceives potential threats everywhere. These threats are often subconscious, or just like the drive to work, we have gotten so used to the tape playing in our head along with the other sixty-thousand thoughts that it seems normal, rote, and routine. We never question limiting thoughts such as: life is hard; the world is dangerous; I am not good enough; people cannot be trusted; there is not enough; I am not safe; they will judge me; they won't like me; and the host of other limiting thoughts and beliefs that invades our brains throughout the day. Operating from this paradigm, everyone we encounter is subconsciously divided into two categories, either friend or foe. It becomes a perpetual self-fulfilling prophecy as we seek out evidence to validate our limiting beliefs. Thereby effectively creating what we fear the most.

Because my emotional needs were not met during the attachment phase of my development, I learned to deny my own needs or to meet them myself and not depend on anyone else. I wouldn't ask for help with anything because I felt no one really cared enough about me to help. As a child I was often called strong-willed and stubborn because I would rather fail at something than to ask for help. My grandmother told me that when I was around age four, I taught myself how to tie my shoes. She said I refused to let anyone help me and I would start crying and protest if someone tried to help me. I do not remember this happening, but I do remember always feeling like I should know things even if I had not been taught. I was deathly afraid of being mocked or punished for being wrong or looking stupid.

On my son's first day of pre-k, he panicked and started crying as we were walking into the building. When I asked him what the matter was, he told me he did not want to go to school because he couldn't read or write. I lovingly explained to him that it was okay that he couldn't read or write and the reason for going to school was so the teacher could teach him how. I assured him he was very smart and that he would be reading and writing very soon. But inside I cringed because I recognized myself in him.

Even now, I sometimes feel a sense of panic when someone tries to help me do something that I think I should do for myself (which is almost everything). A stranger holding a door open or offering to help me with my bags creates an automatic resistance and it is only with practice have I been able to graciously accept these simple courtesies. My childhood home was an abusive and unsafe space. Failures or mistakes were dangerous because it meant being ridiculed or brutally punished. So not only did I need to know how to do things, I needed to know how to do them perfectly.

Once when I was around age nine, I had what could have been described as a panic attack. At the time all I knew was I couldn't breathe, and I felt like I was dying. I was triggered by one of my mother's boyfriends who had been making sexual comments and gestures at me when no one was around. I was terrified of this man, and I avoided him at all costs. But it was Christmas morning, and I was standing at the door of my mother's bedroom. While she was issuing orders to me to clean up the living room, he made a lewd gesture with his tongue at me while lying in bed next to my mother. My mother did not see him, but I did. It felt like I was kicked in the stomach and all the air left my body. I started gasping for air, asking for help, saying I couldn't breathe. The harder it was to breathe the more I panicked. I couldn't dare say what happened to cause this reaction. It was my secret shame, I felt so dirty and so bad. By now I knew for certain that I would be blamed for doing something wrong. I had enough evidence that I was not safe, and I wouldn't be supported.

I can still see myself wide eyed, hands at my throat sweating profusely – surely, they could see I was dying, and they would save me. But instead, my mother started yelling *at me* for being overly dramatic. She said, "If you couldn't breathe you wouldn't be talking. You are so damn dramatic. All you want is attention. Go sit down somewhere." One of my brothers said, "go and run around the house and see if you can catch your breath and I hope you die trying." Another brother said, "Yes, go die." They were laughing *at me*. I went outside and cried alone. When I finally calmed down, I vowed that day I would rather die than ever ask anyone for help. Clearly, they did not care if I died, because they did not care about me, I was on my own. The fighter in me that had helped me to survive up to that point took over. The helpless little girl was already long gone. I wouldn't ask for help with anything – no matter how trivial, and I became quite efficient at being self-reliant. I now know that just because my family of origin did not help or support me doesn't mean I was not worthy of help and support. It only means they were incapable of providing it. I have also learned that suppressing our need for help doesn't stop the stress hormones from surging through our bodies. But I didn't have this information at the time and this incident validated my belief that I was unworthy, unlovable, and could only count on myself.

Fighting was a fear response that helped me survive my childhood. At times I was angry, defensive, aggressive, and controlling. I went toe to toe and word for word with my brothers and anyone else for that matter. No matter how many times they knocked me down I got right up. I refused to let them quash my fire. The same applied to my mother. My avoidant attachment style manifested disdain and dislike towards her, and we were in a constant battle. I flippantly said whatever was on my mind without fear of the consequences. As with many of the households in my neighborhood, my mother's primary punishment consisted of whippings with an extension cord - no belts or switches for her. I received so many whippings that I learned how to take the pain and get it over with. It became a battle of wills with my mother as I would often refuse to cry or yell. I learned early to hide my pain and I became a master at self-denial. During these whippings, I would hold my breath and disassociate from my body in much the same manner as when I was being sexually abused.

However, my anger did manifest, and it was often very violent. In addition to brutal fights with my brothers, I would also fight a lot at school. In my mind I was the champion of the underdog, and I would fight any bully that picked on smaller or weaker kids. I didn't even have to know the person being bullied, but if I saw someone teasing or hurting someone, I would jump right into it and dare them to do it to me. Size did not matter because I had no fear of being hurt. My brothers, my mother, and the perpetrators had trained me well. This propensity for physical violence extended beyond my school years into my early adulthood. I didn't have an anger modulator, and I would go from zero to a blind rage in a matter of seconds.

Conversely, when I was not in fight mode, my other major fear response was fawning, especially for those who were hurt or did not seem to be able to take care of themselves, like my younger siblings or smaller kids. I fine-tuned this defense mechanism and as an adult I became a fierce advocate for the marginalized and underserved. It was as though I had a flashing neon sign on my forehead that read "I will take care of you, fix your problems, and meet your needs."

People who give all the time but who are not comfortable with receiving will attract takers. Because of my emotional programming, I was not comfortable with receiving. Takers loved me, and in many ways, I loved them because I felt valuable when I was helping, supportive, and giving. Of course,

> People that give all the time but that are not comfortable with receiving will attract takers.

I invariably ended up feeling hurt, used, and aabandoned, which reinforced my emotional programming, solidified my belief system, and kept me in the psychocycle, Oops I mean the vicious cycle of re-creating my trauma.

I have a painting of myself in my office that was created by my sister Deb, who is a very talented artist. In this painting she typified me as a woman holding the (literal) world above my head. The expression on my face is one of determination, but there is a subtle sadness in my eyes. On top of this world that I am clearly straining to hold up, a woman kneels in prayer. Over the years I have often studied this painting and for a long time I interpreted the woman on top of the world as a separate being that was praying for my strength as I carried an impossible burden. However, in recent years, I have felt that the praying woman is not a separate being, but that she is an extension of myself. The act of praying is a humble and earnest desire for connection, which is my true and vulnerable self that I've tried so hard to hide from the world.

For most of my life, I had what could be described as an aversion to vulnerability. As a therapist and professor of psychology I had an intellectual understanding of vulnerability and its importance in healing and true connection. I was able to teach this to my students and I expected it from my clients. However, in my self-centered uniqueness, none of this applied to me because for me personally, vulnerability implied weakness and it felt dangerous – life threatening dangerous.

I wouldn't dare ask for help or even let people know I needed support in any area of my life. Although I was constantly in the mix of groups of people, internally I was a lone ranger. As a speaker, I was very comfortable on stage and could command an audience of thousands but was not very comfortable with one-to-one interactions. I always considered myself an extrovert, but I loved my company, and I relished my alone time. I realized later in life that I am not the extrovert as I always thought but more of a true ambivert with traits of both extroverts and introverts.

Even beyond my work as a therapist, people always seemed very comfortable getting vulnerable with me in a very short time after meeting. Along with my professional training and my lack of judgment, I am genuinely compassionate and empathetic, which are traits that most people can sense. However, except for very few people, I didn't get truly vulnerable with anyone. Although as a motivational speaker, I shared a lot of the trauma I experienced as a child as well as the horrors of my drug addiction. There is an inherent vulnerability when I share my trauma and my fears to a group, however, rarely do I have an attachment or an agenda for the group. Also, as a speaker, I am passionate and authentically grateful to share the motivational aspect of my transformation and recovery. I feel an authentic awe and gratitude for the life I now have, and this energy often transfers to the audience. This is not always the case in my personal relationships.

As with most of us, we can show up in our professional uniform as highly functioning adults. However, our trauma responses, the limiting beliefs, and the protections we've developed manifest most starkly with those in our personal relationships. There is an emotional attachment and a set of expectations (reasonable or not) in our personal relationships. This means there is a risk of disappointment, loss, or rejection (i.e., danger.). Even after millions of years of genetic evolution, our old brain's primary purpose is to protect, and it doesn't recognize the difference between physical danger or emotional danger.

The core limiting belief that triggered my protections was that I was not worthy, I would be abandoned, I would be a bother, or my value is only in what I could do for you. I was drawn to a helping profession, and I became a community activist and an advocate for the underserved. In my personal relationships I was a caregiver and a rescuer. I helped raise other people's children, I bailed people out of financial trouble, I allowed people down on their luck or going through crisis to move into my home. I was attracted to men based on what I thought their 'potential' might be and I overlooked all that they were in the present. I was the consummate giver; however, I wouldn't ask for anything and I was often very uncomfortable with receiving.

Take a wild guess as to what kind of people I attracted into my life. If you guessed needy people that sucked me dry but couldn't show up for me then you are correct. Most of my relationships were extremely lopsided. This was not just limited to romantic relationships, but I also attracted very needy individuals as friends. My value was in 'what I' could do rather than in 'who I' was. However, the healthier I became, the healthier the people I attracted into my life. I am no longer attracted to needy men that use and abuse women, and they are no longer attracted to me. I am and will always be a natural caregiver. Acts of service is my love language. However, most of the time I am not operating from a deficit hoping that someone else deems me worthy. I now recognize my own worth and my own value. The caveat is 'most of the time.' This process of healing and transformation is about progress and not perfection. There are times that my old brain goes into automatic protect mode. However, I am much more capable of recognizing the warning signs and engaging my cognitive reasoning skills. I have also developed an amazing intimate support system that will call meout on what I might miss because say in the behavioral health arena 'the true definition of insanity is that we believe our own lies.

One thing I am clear about now that I did not understand then was that the people that I attracted into my life did not abandon me or let me down when I needed something because I was undeserving or unworthy. No, what I now understand is that I attracted and was attracted to people who were constitutionally incapable of meeting my needs or showing up for me. Thereby creating self-fulfilling prophecies that validated my core/faulty beliefs.

This emotional programming was a result of my childhood conditioning and the way I related to my parents, my siblings, and my community. As you have probably already deduced, I had a very adversarial relationship with my mother, we were like oil and water.

I was very resentful and angry towards her and at some point, pre-memory, in true avoidant attachment style, I detached from her. As protection I convinced myself that I did not like her and wanted nothing from her but to be left alone. Of course, these were all protections I developed to ease the pain of rejection I felt from her.

However, I had a different trauma response towards my father that manifested itself in semblance of anxious attachment style. I loved my father; he was a handsome and charismatic man – the proverbial life of the party, his presence was magnetic. He was always kind and loving towards me when he did come around and he made me feel special. My father was the love of my mother's life, but she also harbored anger and disdain towards his inability to be present, to be faithful, and to show up as a father. When he came around, she was happy but when he didn't show up, she was bitter and brooding. Just as I did, she accepted the crumbs he offered her from his table, and she was so much nicer and kinder to me when he was around. I felt visible when he was there – a little less of a burden to my mother – and a little more than just a dot in line with the other dots- which I often felt lumped in with my sibling. I would happily run in from outside when he called my name to hand him his pipe, which was only a few feet away from him. I felt so happy and excited when he called me even though it was mostly to cater to him. "Change the tv channel for me baby." "Bring daddy a cup of coffee-you make it just like I like." "Get a comb and come scratch Daddy's scalp." Are you all seeing the emotional programming happening?

I knew from my mother's constant complaints about my father's absence that he had other children. I felt inferior to these unknown siblings because in my child's mind, I was sure they received a lot of my father's love and attention. His visits were sporadic, and they were never when he promised they would be. My brothers tortured me if I was waiting on my father, and he did not show up. I would pray for him to show up so I wouldn't be teased by them. The first acronym I learned was the one my brothers made up about my father. His name was David, and the acronym was DIAL - which stood for David is a liar. This hurt more than anything else they did to me because it was the one thing that made me feel special.

But the truth was, my father did tell lies and he was unavailable most of my childhood. The feelings I had around my father's absence included uncertainty, not feeling good enough or worthy of his time, wondering if he would call or come see, feeling he did not care about me, feeling less than his other children, even though at the time I had no idea who they were. In my community I felt shame and jealousy around my friends who lived with their fathers. These men were like mystical beings to me. I couldn't understand why my father did not show up and as a form of protection I gave up trying. By the time I was around nine or ten, I had successfully moved into an avoidant attachment style as far as he was concerned. I convinced myself that he didn't matter, and I even convinced myself that he was not my real father. I had the same last name as my other siblings, and I convinced myself that their father was also my father. He hardly came around, so I didn't miss what I never had. These thoughts and feelings helped to form my definition of love.

There is an exercise I use in personal development groups. I write the word home on the board and have the group identify characteristics or attributes of their childhood home. When there is substantive list of words such as sad, unsafe, chaotic, lonely, violent, shaming etc., I cross out the word home and I write the word love. There are usually some gaps from the group as they realize for the first time their idea of love and relationships are dysfunctional because their sense of love is based on the dysfunction in their childhood home. We only know what we have learned. If you grow up in a household that only speaks French, you cannot be expected to speak Spanish when you leave the home.

When I was around eight my father and mother got into a big fight. I was sitting on the front porch steps when he stormed out of the house. He had been drinking and he staggered towards the yellow cab that was pulling into our yard. I started crying because I didn't like it when he was drinking. As he was getting in the cab, he looked over his shoulder and told me he would be back soon. It would be years before I saw my father again. But for a long time, whenever I saw a yellow cab, my heart would patter. Is that him? Is he coming back? Does he still love me? Pitter patter went my heart. This anxious pitter patter in my heart – the pining and the longing is what I learn to identify as love. If I did not feel this pitter patter with boys and later men, I was not attracted.

Even as a little girl I could have been described as lovelorn. From my earliest memories I was constantly falling in love with someone, but it was always the wrong one. I was always attracted to the "bad" boy. I wanted the cutest, the most popular boy – the one all the girls wanted. The one with the edge, the one that was not fawning over me. I found well-behaved boys boring no matter how cute. As I got older, I convinced myself this was because I was attracted to challenges. In some ways this was true, but I realized years later in my recovery process I was attracted to the unavailable because it resonated with the experience of both my parents and especially what I believed to be true about men. They can't be trusted, they cheat and tell lies, they will hurt, abandon, and ultimately reject me.

In the beginning of the chase there was always the excitement of getting them to notice me, see me, like me, choose me. The pitter patter of my heart – hoping to be seen as worthy of his time and attention. I consistently compromised myself and my values in the quest to be chosen by unavailable men and always ended up re-creating my trauma and feeling rejected,

> ...it meant my picker was broken and I was subconsciously choosing partners who were not capable of meeting my emotional needs and loving me the way I deserved to be loved. Prophecy fulfilled.

abandoned, unloved, and wounded. These boys and later in life the men I was attracted to constantly affirmed my belief that I was not lovable and not worthy. I did not realize at the time I was attracting partners that created the same emotional experiences I had with my father or growing up in my abusive household, and that I was essentially creating my own self-fulfilled prophecy. Again, I understand today that because I was rejected or treated in an unlovable manner by my relationship choices doesn't mean I am unlovable. It meant my picker was broken and I was subconsciously choosing partners who were not capable of meeting my emotional needs and loving me the way I deserved to be loved. Prophecy fulfilled.

Today I am able to recognize that there was value in my fear response. They protected me, they helped me to survive the trauma of my childhood and a life of addiction and abusive relationships in early adulthood. I eventually grew into a strong, resilient woman committed to helping the marginalized and underserved in our communities. Those are some of the values and positive attributes I developed. However, these fear responses also kept me on the fringe of my own life, fearful and untrusting in relationships. I was plagued by the feeling of not being good enough, and I was perpetually exhausted, constantly trying to do more, be more, caught in a never-ending circle like a hamster on a wheel. Subconsciously seeking validation and trying to get a positive response to the unasked question "Am I lovable now?" It was not until I began to address some of my deep core beliefs that I was able to take breaks off the hamster wheel.

Cognitive distortion is a psychological term that mean nothing more than the lies we tell ourselves that we believe. The lies can be so cunning and insidious that we base our entire world view, how we feel about others, and more importantly how we feel about ourselves on these distortions. Faulty limiting beliefs are based on distorted thinking – not empirical evidence. Cognitive distortions are quite common across the spectrum of humanity. Although our brain is only two percent of our body space it utilizes twenty percent of the body's energy. The brain never rests, it never shuts down and never takes a rest. It is filled with a constant barrage of chatter, often referred to as monkey brain, and most of this chatter is extremely self-centered, self-critical, and self-concerned. We incessantly ruminate about worries and regrets, and a lot of our thoughts are distorted based on our self-centered view. We all experience cognitive distortions from time to time. However, cognitive distortions become problematic when they form the basis of our world view and our core beliefs about ourselves. The following table identifies some of the common cognitive distortions.

Cognitive Distortion	Description
Mind Reading/ Jumping to conclusion	Without any real evidence, you assume that you know what people think and jump to conclusions without thinking it through or checking it out. "She is judging me because I am overweight".
All or Nothing Thinking/Black or White/Polarized Thinking	Viewing situations or people in all-or-nothing terms. An example would be feeling like a complete failure because you did not get the job you applied for. Everything is either all good or all bad. Anything short of perfection is considered a failure.
Fortune Telling/ Negative Prediction of the Future/ Catastrophizing	Negative prediction of the future based on FEAR, not rational evidence. "I made a mistake at work; I am going t lose my job"
Labeling/Over-generalizing	You assign negative traits globally to yourself and others such as everyone is .., they always…, I never…every time
Discounting Positives/Filtering/ Inability to Disconfirm	Very invested in a negative/ limiting belief, usually when it is tied to a sense of self. Will reject evidence or avoid situations that might contradict your negative thoughts. "Oh, it's nothing special"
Overgeneralizing	Assigning a pattern of negativity based on a single incident. (i.e., All men cheat, or all women supervisors are critical and controlling.)
Should(ing)	Interpreting events, people, and yourself on how you think it should or shouldn't be. These judgments are usually based on unreasonable expectations. "My boss should know how I feel"

Blaming/Victim	Focusing on other people or circumstances as the source of your problems or negative feelings. Refusing to take responsibility for changing yourself, because it is someone or something else that is the problem.
Emotional Reasoning	Putting too much stock in your thoughts and emotions as barometers of truth. Thinking it must be true if I feel it. "I feel like no one is going to help, so I am not going to ask."

These cognitive distortions affirm and feed our fears and limiting beliefs. The first step to changing our cognitive distortions is to become more mindful of the thoughts we are thinking. There is now scientific evidence to support the value of mindfulness. Practices such as pausing and taking slow deep breaths while paying attention to our thoughts are very helpful in changing cognitive distortions and faulty beliefs. I would strongly encourage you to practice taking slow mindful breaths for a few seconds several times a day. Practice will prepare you for the times that you are feeling stressful, confused, or negative thinking. It will be much easier to engage your mindful breathing when you make it part of your regular practices. Remember battles are won in practice and executed on the field. Before we can change our beliefs, we must first become aware of what those beliefs are because we cannot move from a place we are not at.

Spend some time listening and paying attention to your thoughts, even if just for a few minutes a day. Most of the sixty-thousand thoughts we think each day are just below our consciousness and they go unchecked with free reign. Bringing your thoughts into your consciousness gives the cognitive reasoning brain an opportunity to examine and challenge the validity of the cognitive distortions. Looking at the previous sample of cognitive distortions which ones do you find yourself using more than others?

Another mindfulness practice to help you to become aware of your thoughts is to practice regular free form writing. Spend a few minutes daily writing every thought that pops into your mind without filtering or judgment. After just three or four minutes you will see the inclinations of your thoughts and you might be surprised at the insight or thoughts you become aware of in just a few minutes. When done regularly free form writing will provide awareness on where your train of thoughts are taking you. If the destination is not life affirming, positive, or uplifting, you will have the power to make a conscious decision to change directions.

Beliefs based on false evidence are problematic because they create cognitive distortions, and we judge and criticize ourselves and others based on this false evidence. It is the lens that colors our world and shapes our self-esteem and self-concept. We judge our insides (how we feel) by other people's outsides (how they appear) and we constantly come up short. From the outside people may seem more secure, happier, and confident, but contrary to what we think we know, we are not mind readers, we do not know how they feel on the inside. Remember most of us have a public uniform, and we are masters at presenting what we want others to see while masking our true feelings.

Another problem with limiting beliefs is that we project our beliefs about ourselves onto others. Rather than confronting fear or challenging the belief, we manifest behaviors to hide our fears. However, due to the insidious nature of fears, they will always manifest in other ways. For instance, feeling less than or unworthy in a relationship will manifest as insecure and clingy or dominating and controlling. It could also manifest as being detached, aloof, or unavailable. We are afraid that others will see in us what we believe to be true about ourselves. If I feel I am not good enough surely others will recognize this, and they will reject me. We keep the cycle of re-creation going by attracting people to us or being attracted to people and situations that confirm this belief.

The major flaw in all the evidence we have compiled is that it usually has nothing to do with our worth or value but is based on the behaviors or belief system of others. I think this bears repeating…. The major flaw in all the evidence we have compiled is that it usually has nothing to do with our worth or value but is based on the behaviors of others. The way you were treated by your parents, teachers, siblings, co-workers, romantic partners, and others, while painful and traumatic, it has nothing to do with you as it relates to your value and your worth but is more about the unhealed places in others. However, you will not be able to recognize this unless you engage the advanced cognitive reasoning

> The major flaw in all the evidence we have compiled is that it usually has nothing to do with our worth or value but is based on the behaviors or belief system of others.

abilities of your frontal lobe to challenge the evidence.

Think about the choices you have made because of your limiting beliefs. What ways have your limiting beliefs prevented you from living fully, from really going after your dreams? What have you lost or given up because of these beliefs? What chances or opportunities have you let slip by because of your fear and limiting beliefs? What about relationships, how have they been affected? How often have you hid your authentic self or compromised yourself in fear of the core belief that you would be rejected if you honored your truth? How many times have you settled for less or accepted unacceptable behaviors because of your limiting beliefs?

What about the words you speak? These are your thoughts using the creative force of words to manifest your beliefs. The thoughts we think and the words we speak have powerful creative energy. Two of the most powerful words in the human language are *I am*. This is because anything you say after *I am*, becomes your truth and it will manifest in your life through your actions. We are subconsciously (and sometimes consciously) affirming negative messages, *there is never enough money, I am always late, or I could never do that*. We say things like "I am always sick," and then wonder why we are always sick. Instead try saying *I am healthy and whole*, even if you are in bed sick – you will send your immune system a message and speed up your healing process. We may say esteem-destroying things like *I am so stupid, I am too fat, I am ugly, or I am boring*.

Many of our negative thinking and negative beliefs came from words that others spoke to us. Early in my career when I walked into the office of my first job in behavioral health there was a poster in the lobby that read "sticks and stones may break my bones, but words will surely kill me." Reading these words created a paradigm shift as it resonated deep within me and immediately canceled out the childhood ditty I often used "sticks and stones may break my bones, but words can never hurt me." I had spent my life up to this point using this little ditty as a form of protection to pretend that I was not hurt by the words of others. When in all reality the words hurt deeply and left lasting scars. This was reinforced by the adults in my life. If someone was crying or upset about being teased or called bad words, the adults would admonish that they were only words and that they couldn't hurt. Even as a child this was confusing for me because the words and name calling did hurt, so in my child mind I reasoned this must be something else that's wrong with me. I can literally remember making the decision not to cry anymore if someone said something hurtful towards me. I learned to hurl insults back or go into fight mode.

Right there sitting in that lobby looking at that poster, I realized the hard truth was my self-concept and faulty beliefs were based largely on the words that were spoken to me in my formative years. *You are ugly, your hair is too kinky, your skin is too dark, you cry too much or you talk too much.* Even more damaging were statements like *you are stupid. it's all your fault, you always make a mess, you make me sick.*

We then began to form opinions about ourselves based on other people's judgments and the words they have spoken to us. We internalize those words and they become part of our faulty belief system. Where we in turn began to speak the same words or even more damaging words to ourselves both consciously and subconsciously.

Imagine growing up in a household where you were constantly affirmed and told daily how much you were loved and wanted and what a joy you were to be around. You were told you were safe and supported. Your parents validated your worth and value constantly. You felt heard and you felt seen. In this household you were constantly reminded that you were powerful, beautiful, and smart, capable of doing whatever you wanted to do. Now imagine, how would your life have been different from hearing the affirming and validating words throughout your childhood? Would you have the same fears you now have? What about your self-concept and your core beliefs, how different would they be? That my friend is the power of words.

We may not have gotten that type of validation in our childhood, but it is not too late. Positive affirmations can be a powerful tool in changing beliefs. However, if your core belief is 'I am not good enough' and you repeated a thousand times a day 'I am good enough' it is not enough to disrupt the neural pathways or truly change your long-held belief of not being worthy. The reason that simply speaking positive affirmations alone do not work is because your core beliefs were not deeply ingrained by repeating over and over, I am not lovable. Your core beliefs are based on evidence gathered through actions and experience.

Positive affirmations plus demonstrated action equals transformation. When coupled with action, affirmations are a powerful tool to utilize when confronting fear and changing limiting beliefs. There is now scientific evidence validating the power of affirmations. Directing your focus and attention on the affirmation sends signals through neural pathways, literally reprogramming the brain. And the evidence shows that they work with both physical and emotional issues.

While writing this book, a tumor was was found in my right breast. These hard calcifications had been popping up in my breast for over thirty years, and this was the sixth tumor. They were all biopsied and found to be benign, but it was extremely discomforting every few years to discover another tumor and to wonder if this is going to be the one that is malignant. They were even more worrisome because I have a family history of cancer, especially breast cancer. I have two sisters who valiantly fought and survived breast cancer. And although it is extremely rare, my youngest brother had breast cancer. He survived the chemo and radiation that killed the cancer, but it took a toll on his heart, and after being in remission, he died of heart failure. One of my brother's daughters was diagnosed with breast cancer at age 21 and is now a miraculous survivor. However, I lost two aunts to their battle against breast cancer. I had my own history with cancer resulting in a complete hysterectomy at age thirty-nine.

However, this sixth tumor discovered in my sixtieth year of life seemed different. And while the biopsy did not determine it to be cancer it was found to be suspicious, which my doctor described as pre-cancerous. Due to my family history of breast cancer, my doctor tested me forthe BRCA gene, which identifies genetic markers that could mutate and significantly increase the risk of breast and ovarian cancer. Not surprisingly, I tested positive for the BRCA-2 gene. It felt as though I had been playing Russian roulette and the odds were stacked against me. My doctor felt that it was not a matter of 'if' but a matter of when.

Several options were presented to me based upon my personal and family history: do nothing; have more frequent mammograms and breast MRIs throughout the year and hope to catch any malignancy early. But there was the issue of my immune system being strong enough to handle high doses of chemo due to an immunocompromising condition I have where my bone marrow doesn't produce enough healthy white cells. Another option offered was to take a daily dose of low-level chemo for the next five to ten years to help decrease the chances of cancer forming (but live with the side effects of low-dose chemo such as experiencing all the symptoms of menopause-again!). And the final option was to have a radical prophylactic double mastectomy to decrease the chance of developing breast cancer by ninety-five percent.

After many medical consultations, my own personal research, speaking with loved ones, talking with my ancestors, praying, and deep soul searching I made the decision to have both my breasts removed as a preventative to developing breast cancer. This was a life shaking, psyche braking, paradigm altering decision, but I chose to fight the fight on this side rather than wait for a cancer diagnosis. In many ways I have been changed forever by this experience, but that will have to be unpacked at a later time, possibly in a future book. I want to circle back to the power of thoughts and the language we speak in shifting our circumstance.

No amount of research or consultations I received pre-mastectomy prepared me for the pain and discomfort I would feel post-surgery. After removing all my breast tissue, including my nipples and areola, expanders were placed into my chest for the purpose of stretching my skin over the next few months to make room to place implants and to provide my now traumatized body with some semblance of normalcy. The radical cutting off of my breast and the pain from the expanders was practically unbearable. For months I had to endure regular injections of saline into the expanders to expand what was left of the skin and muscles that once housed my breast. For weeks I languished on my couch, unable to lay flat in my bed and I was in the worst physical pain of my life. I found myself saying over and over to myself and anyone that would listen, *I am miserable, I am in so much pain, this is too much, why did I do this to my body, I'm scared.* This went on and on. Finally, the knowledge and the wisdom I had been downloading into my psyche for years kicked back in. I was reminded of the power of thought and the manifesting power of the spoken word.

I began to speak positively to myself and others by constantly saying things like, *I am good, I am well, I am vibrant and healthy, my body is beautiful and perfect.* I began to honor the pain as part of my body's healing process, and I began to acknowledge and honor the warrior spirit in me that made the empowered choice to have this procedure.

I didn't pretend that the pain or the trauma was not there. But once I acknowledged its value, I changed my relationship with the pain, and my healing process became so much more bearable. The same applies for your emotional pain and the traumas you have experienced. It happened and it exists. No positive affirmations or positive thinking will change that. However, you can use words and thoughts to change your relationship to the pain or trauma, create new neural pathways in your brain, and transform your life.

Some practical ways to use affirmations are:

- Use the creative energy of words to call those things that are not into existence.
- Always speak affirmations in the present tense, for instance, do not say, "I will be okay," say "I am okay."
- Always infer something positive, do not say, "I am not fat," rather affirm, "I am healthy and whole."
- Make your affirmations short phrases that are easily repeated throughout the day.
- Write them on sticky notes and stick them everywhere – mirror, fridge, wallet, car console, your computer, eventually just seeing the sticky note will trigger thoughts of your affirmation.

- Create life-affirming thoughts such as, "I am lovable, I am enough, I am worthy, I am prosperous, and I am healthy and whole."
- Choose one affirmation and stick with it for at least a week. Say it to yourself (aloud if possible) as many times as possible. Try saying it a thousand times a day – when you consider we think about sixty thousand thoughts a day this is not a lot.
- **Think about what you are thinking about**. Become aware of the negative self-talk and began to replace it with positive life affirming thoughts.
- Spend a few minutes repeatedly invoking your affirmation each morning upon waking, again in the middle of the day, and in the evening before going to sleep. Also, say it throughout the day.
- Your words and actions have the power to reprogram your brain. Change your words, and your relationship with yourself will change.
- Change the relationship with yourself and you will change your relationship with others.
- Some example affirmations are:
  - I am lovable
  - I am safe
  - I am worthy
  - I am enough
  - I am lovingly supported
  - I am protected by divine presence
  - I am making healthy choices
  - I am whole and healthy
  - I am great to be around
  - I am strong and powerful
  - I am beautiful
  - I am prosperous
  - I am courageous
  - I am brave
  - I am smart
  - I am confident
  - I am calm and peaceful
  - I am good

Choose an affirmation and write it at least seven times on separate sticky notes. Post those notes throughout your house (bathroom mirror, fridge, etc.) car, office, wallet, or anywhere you will see them regularly throughout the day and repeat as often as possible.

Feeling small, unimportant, or unlovable has its advantages. It becomes a good excuse for not following your dreams or taking risks, settling for mediocre or even settling for less. Your limiting beliefs can create a safe place void of any expectations, responsibility, or accountability. But there is something in you that wants more. If this were not true, you wouldn't still be reading this book.

Yes, you may fail, you may be rejected, but then again you may not. Take the risk and trust that if you do fail, if you are rejected, that you are perfectly capable of handling disappointments and taking care of yourself. You are no longer a child dependent upon angry, cold, or inconsistent giants to meet your needs. You can meet your own needs now with love and compassion.

All living things seek growth and evolution. Just as the seed pushes forth in the dark and damp dirt, so do humans. We naturally seek growth, to learn, to change, to evolve. This is part of the living process; from the second we are born, there is a natural evolution to life. Understand there is a difference between personal development and fixing ourselves. You are not broken therefore you do not need to be fixed. There is nothing wrong with the caterpillar. The transformation to a butterfly is simply what happens when the caterpillar has outgrown its current state. Once you shed the distorted thinking and faulty beliefs you may be surprised what you find when you look for the PURPLE. You have always been enough, you have enough, there is enough.

> There is nothing wrong with the caterpillar. The transformation to a butterfly is simply what happens when the caterpillar has outgrown its current state.

The following exercise can help you change your cognitive distortions and limiting beliefs.

- In column 1 write your negative thoughts or cognitive distortions.

- In column 2 identify what you think is the underlying assumption or limiting beliefs.

- In column 3 Identify the positive affirmation you will use to counter limiting thoughts and beliefs.

- In column 4 (This is very important.) Identify the actions you will take to confirm the affirmation.

Negative Thought/ Cognitive Distortion	Underlying Assumption/ Limiting Belief	Positive Affirmation to Counter Limiting Thoughts/ beliefs	Action to Confirm Affirmation

Chapter Five

Rational Evidence Annihilates Lies (REAL)

Again, let us repeat the truth. You are good enough, you are worthy, and you are absolutely lovable. You are a manifestation of life experiencing itself through you. Whether you believe this or not doesn't make it any less true. I understand you have gathered a lifetime of evidence to the contrary. But it is false evidence. You have felt less than, not pretty enough, not smart enough, not athletic enough, not competent enough, and not anything else you have added to your fear-based arsenal of false evidence. Feelings are not facts, and a belief is nothing more than

> It is part of our inherent self-centeredness that we automatically give credence to our thoughts and rarely do we challenge the validity of our own thinking.

what you tell yourself is true. Just because you tell yourself it is true, doesn't make it true. It is part of our inherent self-centeredness that we automatically give credence to our thoughts and rarely do we challenge the validity of our own thinking. But challenge it you must.

Remember the baby you imagined earlier in the book? That baby is who we all were at some point and who we still are at our core. We may have had challenging experiences along the way. We may have shame, guilt, regret, and remorse. We have all made mistakes and we may have caused harm to others - sometimes intentionally. The historical archives and the world's prisons are full of people that have done horrific things, including crimes against humanity. Yet no matter who we turned into as adults we were all that baby once innocent and with a natural need for love and support. Perhaps he or she was a baby that did not get his or her needs met or that experiences horrible trauma. It is natural to begin to close off our hearts to protect ourselves from further emotional wounding. In the process of building up and fortifying our protections to keep others from hurting us, we may end up imprisoning ourselves.

But who among us is not deserving of compassion and love? If I were to be judged for only my mistakes, I wouldn't stand the test of the trial, but would have long since been banished. I am grateful that instead of justice I have received grace. Just as you are much more than the mistakes you have made so aren't we all. I am convinced the world would be a better place and we would have much more empathy and compassion for ourselves and others if we could see us all as the innocent baby and the wounded child we once were.

You are still as worthy as that baby, and this immutable truth cannot be changed by a faulty belief system. No matter how the false evidence tries to convince you otherwise. The false evidence that forms the basis of your limiting beliefs must be annihilated with concrete, rational evidence that contradicts the faulty beliefs. Pay attention to your judgments and examine them for they are part of your limiting belief system.

There is tangible evidence in your life right now that speaks to your worthiness. In this case, participating in personal development by reading this book is real evidence. You wouldn't be reading this book unless there was a part of you that recognized your worth. It is a tangible action providing solid proof, not just a thought or belief. You may not always arrive at the real evidence of this easily, and you may have to peel off layers of doubt, confusion, and misinformation to get to the truth, but the truth is there waiting to be found. You do not even need to believe your healing is possible or that the principles in this book work. The proof is in practice - practice them and you will retrain your brain. Build your expectancy on actual outcomes in your life. Do not give up, do not stop seeking. I promise you if you look hard enough for the PURPLE, you will find it. It is everywhere and it has always been everywhere.

As most psychological theories suggest, most of our faulty beliefs got locked and loaded in early childhood. I have found in my work with individuals and groups that there is sometimes a tendency to dismiss the influence of our childhood experiences on our adult life. This may be because we naturally process our childhood experiences through our adult brain with its cognitive reasoning abilities. As an adult it is easier to understand and dismiss the dysfunction of your childhood home.

I cannot count the number of times I've heard individuals discount the harsh beatings and punishments of their childhood by surmising that most of their childhood peers were punished the same, or by believing the dysfunctional rationale that the beatings helped them to turn out okay. We have so much more knowledge and experience than we did as a child. Our adult brain now understands mental illness, addictions, and generational dysfunction. However, we did not have this brain as children and while it makes their behavior understandable it doesn't minimize the effect it had in developing a faulty belief system. I doubt if there is a child anywhere on the planet being brutally whipped by a parent that is thinking 'my parent really loves me, and this is going to help me be a better person.'

On the flip side, being able to understand our parents as adults helps with the healing process. It is easier to understand or have compassion for our parents once we become parents or after we have made a few mistakes of our own. When I became a mother, I had much more compassion and understanding for my mother. She literally had ten times the number of children I had, and I cannot not phantom how she coped with all our personalities and behaviors.

As I have mentioned a few times already, my son was really a great kid. I rarely had to discipline him, and when I did, I used age-appropriate essays as a disciplinary tool because I felt he should learn something rather than just be punished. Starting at around age six in response to him not following instruction given by my sister with an essay on 'why I need to listen to my aunt' all the way through school and his final essay in response to him joking around too much in class on 'why my education is important to the rest of my life.' These essays were an effective means for him to think critically about his behavior.

However, as mundane as it sounds, he and I had a constant power struggle for years over him taking out the trash. I would get so frustrated because no matter how much I reminded him he couldn't seem to remember, or he chose to forget that every Tuesday and every Friday the trash can needed to go to the curb. How hard could it be to remember that? When he was in his early teens, and testing his autonomy, I said to him "The trash can needs to go out to the curb." Later when I realized he had not taken the trash to the curb I angrily confronted him about it. His response was "You told me the trash needed to go out to the curb. You did not tell me to take the trash out." I felt the anger rising in my throat and I saw a flash of me grabbing him by his collar and throwing him out his bedroom window. I told him to get the trash out now, and I stormed away before I did or said something I would regret.

As I marched downstairs, my first thought was how did my mother manage with a house full of kids. I only had one child and I just had the urge to throw him out of a window. No wonder she was angry and frustrated all the time. In that moment I had such compassion for my mother because now as a mother, I was able to relate as a mother. My mother was a single mom, struggling to make ends meet while dealing with overwhelming socio-economic issues with a house full of children and there there were a couple of us who were unable and unwilling to be still or quiet. I for one prided myself on constantly having something smart-alecky to say back to my mother. I suddenly saw myself as a child through my son and I wanted nothing more than to give my mother a hug. However, I was only able to do this through my adult brain and my experiences as a mom.

We must remember that this brain, reasoning abilities, and experiences did not exist in our early childhood. The primitive brain ran the show and on an emotional level it may still be running the show. While there is evidence to back up this claim as a scientific fact, most of us do not need science to tell us this, because we have experienced the old brain's ability to hijack our thinking brain in 1.2 seconds. To change fear-based limiting beliefs you must confront them by fully engaging your thinking brain and limiting input from your old or mid brain.

Stop, take a few deep breaths and challenge the belief. Hold it up to the light of what is REAL (Rational Evidence Annihilates Lies) Is it really true? Challenge it. Am I really not worthy? I know it may feel true but engage your logic and critical thinking adult brain. Identify rational evidence that contradicts this faulty belief. This new evidence must be real and undeniable evidence to annihilate the lies. Remember, your primitive brain has millions of years of genetic inclination towards prioritizing threats and negativity. You cannot half-heartedly engage your false beliefs. Therefore, your new evidence must be specific rather than general. 'I am a good mother' or 'I help others" is not specific enough'. Your old and mid brain has a lifetime of practice denying the existence of PURPLE.

> This new evidence must be real and undeniable evidence to annihilate the lies. Remember, your primitive brain has millions of years of genetic inclination towards prioritizing threats and negativity.

"I joined a group of parents for mutual support and guidance, and it is helping me be a better parent. This is important to me because I am breaking the cycle of generational dysfunction." This statement is more specific and harder to contradict. You wouldn't engage in personal development unless there is a part of you that know you deserve to be your best you. The evidence is there, search for it. Look for the PURPLE.

What other tangible actions have you taken that demonstrate you are worthy? The answer could be, "I get up at 6:00 AM to work out because my body is worth being taken care of" or "I am reading this book because I want to be a better person, I want to change my limiting belief system." "Why?" "Because I deserve to live a more fulfilling life." "Why?" "Because I am worth it." "Wait, because you are worth it?" How do you know this?" "Because I feel it right now from deep within myself. I am worthy. No matter what others thought of me or how they treated me. I am worthy." Yes, you are worthy.

Your worth is not defined by the behaviors of others – no matter what they said or what they did it doesn't determine your worth. Their behavior says more about their wounding and their need for healing than it does about your value.

You are now an adult, and you no longer need to be held hostage by the behaviors of others. As a child I couldn't do anything about my abuse, I was powerless. Our brains are not fully developed until we are well into our twenties. As children, not only is our developing brain extremely impressionable, but we have no control over our family of origin or the adverse experiences of our childhood. In so many ways we were helpless and powerless. But as adults we are no longer powerless. We can reprogram our brain, and not only change our belief system, but we can literally change the physiology of our brain. Now that's real power. It is a new day, and the day of hopeless suffering is over. Step into this new day determined to challenge and change your limiting beliefs.

Challenge your FEARs with what is REAL. What is the rational evidence? What do you know to be good and to be true about yourself? Write these questions down and write your response so you can see them in your own handwriting which further strengthens new learning and helps to create new neural pathways. Keep the document easily accessible for whenever you need to be reminded of your R.E.A.L. truth. If you are going down, you might as well go down swinging a broom.

It is the willingness to challenge our long-held beliefs and to take an honest inventory of ourselves that helps us to discover the PURPLE in our lives. It is self-defeating and martyrdom to only look at the negative and the brown in our lives, and it creates unnecessary suffering. We are all flawed with shortcomings, idiosyncrasies, and quirks that make us individuals. But that is just part of who we are, and it doesn't take away our power. One of my favorite quotes comes from Marianne Williamson's A *Return to* Love "Our deepest fear is not that we are inadequate. Our deepest fear is that we are powerful beyond measure. It is our light, not our darkness that most frighten us." You are

> You are powerful beyond measure. You have the power to literally reshape and reprogram your brain. And you can do this not over years but within weeks of intentional consciousness and reframing. That is power. In fact, that is a superpower!

powerful beyond measure. You have the power to literally reshape and reprogram your brain. And you can do this not over years but within weeks with intentional consciousness and reframing. That is power. In fact, that is a superpower!

Looking for the PURPLE focuses your attention on your light and what is good in your life, which ignites your brain's superpower. What scares you the most about finding your PURPLE and letting your light shine? Playing small, not being your authentic self, hiding your talents and gifts, and not living in your purpose and power doesn't serve you or anyone else. Our limiting beliefs serve the purpose of keeping us safe and comfy. Change is scary and the familiar is safe. No matter how toxic the familiar is there is a certain comfort in the familiar. Change takes us out of this comfort zone and outside of the comfort zone is uncomfortable, which can bequite scary. But as one of my favorite axiom states, "If you don't have any fear in your life, you are living way too small."

What would you need to change if you let go of your limiting beliefs? What relationships would no longer serve you if you really honored your truth? Are you willing to let those relationships go? It is often the fear of change that keeps us holding to the negative belief. Fully embracing our power, our worthiness, and our loveliness means we can no longer continue to stay the same, a victim of other people's behavior or a victim of our own story. If you are going to tell the story, tell the whole story. Do not share the bad things about your childhood without sharing about the good. Do not leave out the parts about your power and resiliency. Are you willing to let go of your attachment to the pain and the trauma? Life is energy – everything alive must move and evolve, or the process of death begins. You are now in the process, continue to move forward.

Let us review the emotional programming illustration but this time we are going to add the REAL acronym.

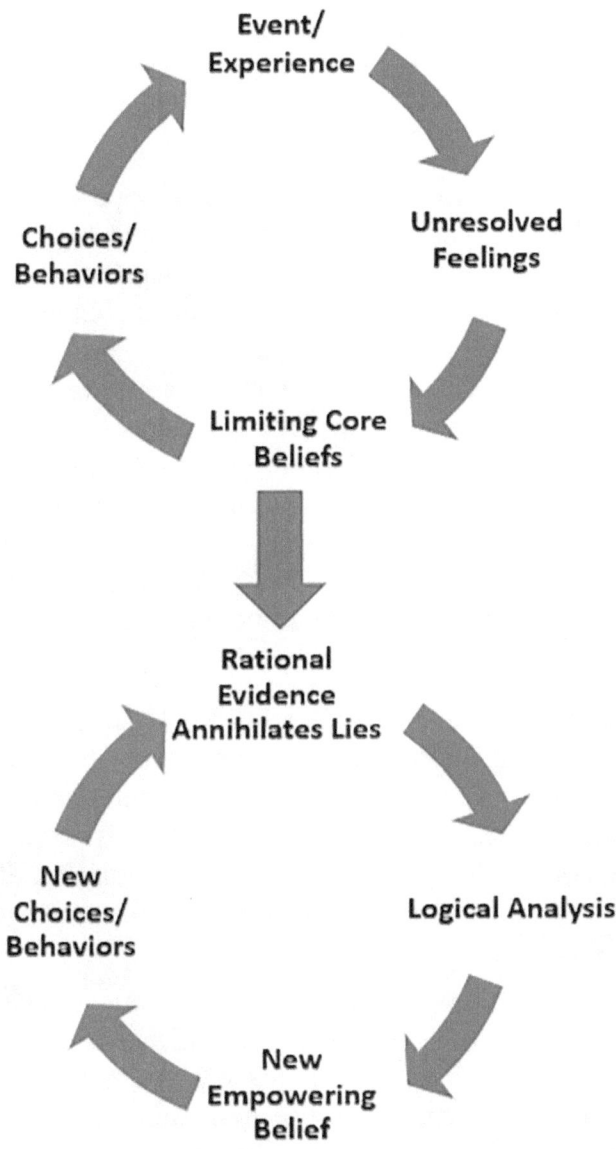

Once while I was serving on a jury, we received instructions from the judge that were simple yet poignant. He stated to the jury that it doesn't matter how we felt – but that we must only consider the evidence – not our emotions. During deliberations we were able to hold each other accountable when someone mentioned they felt the police officer involved in the case was being unfair and a few of us said in unison – but we must only consider the evidence? This was a valuable lesson to me regarding evidence-based critical thinking. We need this same practice to annihilate the lies and to determine what is REAL in our lives.

The following exercise provides you with an opportunity to challenge your faulty beliefs with rationale evidence and logical analysis so that you may begin to create new beliefs that are strengthened and validated by new actions. After completing the exercise, I strongly encourage you to spend at least the next seven days gathering an arsenal of evidence that validates your new empowering belief. Keep a journal and write down every piece of evidence you find no matter how small or seemingly trivia – a compliment from a stranger, a C on a test when you thought you were going to fail, an act of self-care – write it all down. After seven days continue to search for evidence – at least one solid piece of evidence every day. The more you look the easier it is to find and the more you find the easier it is to believe.

Column 1 – False Evidence Appearing Real – In this column begin to identify your limiting beliefs. By now you should have a pretty good idea of what those are. If not, do a quick free form writing exercise with the prompt: "my limiting beliefs are…" It's okay if you are not able to recognize all of your limiting beliefs, just write the ones that are coming to the surface (as those are the ones that are most ready to be healed).

Column 2 – Rational Evidence – Identify the rational evidence that is in your life right now. Believing the evidence is not a requirement right now. As much as you can, leave your emotions out of it. You are on a fact-finding mission, use your adult brain and simply state the facts, no matter what the emotions are saying. Remember your emotions are often based on your faulty beliefs.

Column 3 – Logical Analysis – This is where the fun begins. Pretend you are a lawyer in a courtroom, and that you must convince the jury the evidence being presented is false and convince them beyond a shadow of doubt of the real evidence. What would you say? Keep in mind the instructions given to jurors...decide the case only on the presented evidence – no emotions allowed. Write down your logical analysis, further sealing it into your thought process.

Column 4 – New Empowering Beliefs – Based on your logical analysis, what is your new empowering belief. Hint: it is usually just the opposite of the limiting beliefs. Write the new beliefs as "I am" affirmations on at least seven sticky notes, post them in visible locations, and repeat often throughout your day.

Column 5 – New Choices/New Behaviors - This is a critical step in the process. What new choices and/or behaviors will you engage in to validate and solidify your new belief? Do you need to ask for a raise, enroll in school, or set boundaries in a relationship? It's okay if there is fear. Feel the fear and take the action anyways. Maybe you won't get the raise or maybe you will be rejected. That is not as important as it is that you demonstrate your value and worthiness to yourself. Even if denied you are setting neurons in motion and creating new neuropathways. Remember neurons that fire together wire together.

(1)	(2)	(3)	(4)	(5)
False Evidence Appearing Real	Rational Evidence	Logical Analysis	New Empowering Belief	New Choices/ Behaviors

Chapter Six

There is PURPLE in the Pain

Folklore considers the lotus flower to be a revered and sacred flower symbolizing resiliency. This beautiful flower grows from the muddy bottom of the pond where little else should be able to survive. But, reaching for the sunlight through the mud and murky water, the beautiful blossom appears. Seemingly untouched by its sullied beginnings and surroundings, the lotus blossom represents resiliency, strength, and the ability to not only survive but to thrive in the bleakest of circumstances. The lotus blossom reminds me of the beauty that exists within all of us alongside the pain and the trauma. As we reach for the light of truth, compassion, and love, we can see beauty that is as much a part of who we are as our pain. The two are not mutually exclusive. Look for the PURPLE in your life. I believe that recognizing this beauty while honoring our pain helps us to find purpose.

Pain is part of the body's survival system. Just as fear keeps us safe from real and present danger, imagine a life where there wasn't any pain. We need the boundaries that are set by feeling pain. If we didn't feel the pain from the heat of the fire, we would destroy ourselves. This applies to emotional pain as well. It helps us to set boundaries that are necessary for our emotional survival.

In his timeless classic The Prophet, author Kahil Gibran describes pain by writing, "Your pain is the breaking of the shell that encloses understanding. Even as the stone of the fruit must break, that its heart may stand in the sun, so must you know pain." Pain appears to be an inevitable part of life; however, we have been pre-disposed with the innate ability to survive, adapt, and thrive from our pain.

One of the best ways to honor our experiences and our process is to transform our pain into something positive. This gives our pain value and adds purpose and passion to our lives. The Latin origin of the word passion means to suffer. Show me someone that is extremely passionate about a cause, and I will show you someone that has experienced pain related to that cause. Purpose transforms that pain into something meaningful. For my son it is art. For me I choose to work in the behavioral health field to help others transform their lives. Utilizing my trauma and my experiences to help others gives value and adds purpose to my pain.

For many years, I taught a college course on Positive Psychology. Unlike most tenets of psychology that focused on pathology, positive psychology focuses on human resiliency, strength, and joy. This relatively new school of thought is now bolstered by the science of brain scans and neurofeedback. There is now empirical evidence supporting the benefits of positive psychology attributes such as optimism, happiness, empathy, and gratitude.

My favorite principle of positive psychology is the resiliency factors known as post-traumatic growth syndrome. Unlike post-traumatic stress syndrome (PTSD), post-traumatic growth is the resiliency, strength, and growth that is developed as a result of personal trauma or adverse experiences. It goes beyond 'surviving' trauma to 'thriving' and even benefiting from the trauma. Post traumatic growth is the proverbial 'if life hands you lemons make some really delicious lemonade' or another one of my favorite sayings to describe resiliency is 'turn stumbling blocks into steppingstones' I recently received an inspirational quote from a friend that read, "Strength isn't about how much you can handle before you break, but it is about how much you can handle after you have been broken." It is the ability to learn from our pain and integrate it into something positive.

Again, trauma is subjective and what could be considered trauma is as varied as there are humans on the planet. As stated previously, I did not understand the depth to which certain events affected my son. Most parents do not. When he was around four years of age, I missed another adverse event that shaped his life. We were at our local mall, and he was playing at the little indoor playground, which was his favorite thing to do at the mall. He would go up and down that little slide for hours if allowed, and I always made sure he had a few minutes to enjoy playing on the little slides and running in out of the little tunnels. On this day, I was in no hurry, so I purchased a lemonade and settled myself on the bench to watch him play. Watching my son play with abandonment was one of my greatest joys as a mother. His elation and abandonment of his play always filled me with such a sense of gratitude, peace, and contentment. There is a greeting in certain African tribes that translate to "How are the children?" I understand the sentiment of this greeting because if the children are okay – if they are happy and if they are well, then so is the family, and so is the village.

As I watch my son gleefully run around that tiny playground, I feel the joy and contentment of "Yes,the children are well." At this point, a mall security guard approached me with a stern expression on his face and stated somewhat aggressively that my son was not allowed to play on the playground because he was too old. I was taken aback by his confrontational manner, and I remarked to him that my son was only four years old. He looked at me in disbelief and countered with "Well, he is awfully tall for four. As he stated this he walked over and stood next to a statue of a little elf holding a scroll that measured height. This scroll marked the height limitation for this playground. The security guard practically shouted, it doesn't matter how old he is because it is only the height that matters. He did this in a dramatic fashion as though he was presenting surprise evidence in a courtroom, as he pointed out that my son was taller than the measuring scroll allowed.

My son was taller than most four-year-olds. But was this hostile man standing in front of me serious? I told him again that my son was only four, but he simply shrugged and smugly stated, "Age don't matter, only height and the inches on this scroll." Seriously? Was his job that boring or his life so miserable that he found delight in harassing preschoolers on a mall playground?

At this point Shaka had stopped playing and was looking at the security guard and little elf scroll with a confused expression. He then looked at me and stated pleadingly "But Mommy, I fit fine, I am not too tall to play." At this point, I feel my anger rising into my throat and I made a choice not to waste my energy arguing with an obviously miserable man. Much to Shaka's dismay, I took hm by the hand and marched off. He started crying because he did not understand why the police said he was too tall to play when he was playing just fine. My anger increased when I realized he thought that mall security was a police officer. As the mother of a Black son there is a rational trepidation at the thought of my son interacting with a police officer. I knew I would have "the talk" that most Black parents have with their kids regarding interacting with police officers. Unfortunately, it is a standard 'talk' that probably happens in most Black households, especially with Black boys. We caution them to be polite, say yes sir, no sir. No matter how unfair the stop is, your goal is to make it home alive. But I did not expect this interaction to occur at such a young age and certainly not in the form of mall security. However, my way of addressing this situation was to tell my son that he did not need the mall playground because he had one in his backyard. Even though I knew the little swing set in our backyard did not measure up to the jungle gym at the mall playground. I also knew the jungle gym was not the issue, but I chose to ignore the bigger issue. My son knew it too, and he wouldn't be consoled, crying himself to sleep in the backseat on the ride home. In my mind that was the end of that. It felt like a seemingly harmless event, with an overzealous mall cop.

Shaka would grow to be 6'6", slightly taller than his father. He would always be the tallest kid in the class, park, etc. and people constantly remarked about his height. By age five, he was enrolled in a community basketball program. Because he was so tall, I assumed he would grow up playing basketball like his dad. By the time he reached middle school, he made it clear he was no longer interested in playing basketball but would rather spend all his free time on his skateboard. I was disappointed because I had an expectation that he would play basketball. However, I yielded my hopes for him playing basketball and supported him in his choice of extracurricular activities.

Shortly after he quit playing basketball, I noticed how irritable he became when he was asked "You play ball?" or, without even asking if he played basketball, total strangers would ask what position he played. My son would often respond in a deadpan manner, "Why do you think I play basketball?" This usually made the asker uncomfortable, and they would usually justify their question by remarking on his height. More bolder adults would tell my son that he should be playing basketball, as though he was wasting his height and body by not doing so.

My son was not going to be a basketball star. However, he was brilliant, creative, articulate, funny, caring, and conscious. I was heavily involved in the community both through work and volunteering and Shaka often accompanied me and helped at volunteer events. I worked in programs that served the homeless, drug addicted, and criminal justice involved individuals, and he spent plenty of after school hours at my job. Because he was exposed to and closely involved in social services his entire life, he was compassionate and kind. Once we were driving downtown and saw a homeless man pushing a shopping cart filled with all his worldly possessions down the street when my son suddenly shouted gleefully, "Hi, Thomas!" from the car window. He recognized Thomas from the homeless shelter where he volunteered serving meals, and Thomas seemed happy to see him as he excitedly waved back. My son was quite a kid, and I couldn't be prouder as a mom. And while I celebrated his many accomplishments, I was prouder of who he was as a human being.

I felt the constant comments about his height disregarded who he was as a person. I too, became offended by the assumption others made about his height and basketball, and I would flippantly respond with my own version of "why do you think he should be playing basketball, daring them to state the obvious truth that was contained in their statement?" Both Shaka and I understood these stereotypical assumptions were based on his height and his race – and they minimized my brilliant and caring son's gifts and talents.

Back to the mall playground experience, I would soon learn the traumatic effect it had on my son. After the security guard incident, whenever we went to that mall and walked past the playground, Shaka would always make a comment about being too tall to play there. Because of the humor he attached to it, I did not think much of it, and it became a little inside joke. He would say something like 'play little children, but pay attention to that elf, because soon will be the day that you will be no longer allowed in there,' and we would laugh.

By the time he was a teenager he would playfully snarl at the sight of the playground. When he went away to college, I would get random photos of the little elf or some other creature holding the inch ruler at a mall playground somewhere with the caption "never forget". I would always laugh at his humor and what I thought was our inside joke.

However, I would later learn that Shaka used this humor to deal with his pain. This pain began to manifest on that little mall playground. His was the pain of not being seen. Many psychological theories posit that being ignored or not being seen is just as traumatic to a child as physical abuse. Children's self-concept and self-esteem is developed based on their interactions with their environment, especially their interactions with parents, teachers, and other authority figures. Many of the adults in Shaka's environment did not see him. They saw his height and they saw his skin color. They did not see him. They did not care how intelligent or creative he was, they saw a tall Black male that 'should' be playing basketball.

His first year of college he really struggled in developing his autonomy and figuring out where he fit. It didn't help that he attended a university with one of the best basketball teams in the country. He received a lot of well-meaning but hurtful feedback from everywhere while at Florida State regarding him joining their basketball team. As brilliant as he was, he began to struggle academically. He had chosen political science as a major and decided he was going to become a lawyer. He was not excited about his major but chose it because he thought it was expected of him 'to do something great for his community.' He was miserable and nearly flunked out of college in his first year. It wasn't until he took a writing class that he found his joy. He was a brilliant creative writer and he excelled academically after he changed his major to English.

Shaka went to graduate school where he received a master's in fine arts. He was able to articulate his pain and the trauma of invisibility into his passion for art. He brilliantly utilized film and mixed media to examine the stereotyping and commodifying of the Black male body in his master thesis titled: "You Play Ball?" He encased the basketball of his childhood in acrylic resin, forever turning it into an art as a response to the question 'you play ball?'. His filmed showcased him shooting one thousand free throws from two different angles. The wide angle showed him and the entire court as he shot free throw after free throw. Each shot was loaded with reactions from hope, disappointment, satisfaction, failure, determination, and fear in a never-ending loop. The close-up angle was only of his face as he sweated and struggled free throw after free throw, highlighting the labor and hard work was the fun of the game. It was a three-hour loop, played nonstop on two large screens for two weeks at his college's downtown Boston campus, the window of which faced a busy street, inviting those passing by to participate as a spectator in the struggle of the game. It was poignant and powerful in its representation of the futile attempt of young Black men that are often told becoming an athlete is their only way out of impoverished communities. To represent the commodification, he created five different trading cards that depicted five non-athlete aspects of him: English Major, Graduate Student, Musician, Fine Artist, and Film Maker. My son was healing his pain and challenging the stereotype that had been placed on him through his art.

This was just the beginning of him using basketballs in his art. After graduate school, he applied to an Artist in Residence program at the Boston Center for the Arts. Out of the applications submitted from all over the city Shaka was chosen for this prestigious residency. His proposal for a community art project was to involve the community by holding basketball drives throughout underserved communities in Boston. He invited the community to donate new basketballs and he invited kids to exchange their old basketballs for new ones. He donated new basketballs to the Boys & Girls Club, where he held art classes with children using the old basketballs as a canvas. He then took these wonderfully and joyfully decorated basketballs and created an outdoor sculpture using milk crates (often used in poorer communities as a basketball hoop). This semi-permanent sculpture was on display in front of the Boston Center for the Arts for months. He included the names of the children who created the art on the basketballs as contributors to the sculptor. Children from all over the city could come and see their name as part of this art project while they interacted with the sculpture by playing, swinging, or sitting on it. But more importantly, for children in the underserved communities, they could now reimagine the use of a basketball and see art as part of their personal story.

The project gained a lot of media attention and opened many doors for my son including NBA teams soliciting him to do a similar project in other locations or being selected by Converse to model their new basketball shoes. There were many interviews and many articles written. However, the most impactful for me was an article in an art magazine where he shared how it really affected his psyche growing up "too tall" – a throwback reference to the mall cop. He stated how he often felt less than or that he was 'wasting' his height (i.e., his life) by not playing basketball. The magazine quoted him saying, "it really hurts when everyone is telling you that you should be playing basketball because of your height – especially your own parents." When I read that quote, the sum of all his experiences since that day at the mall playground hit me smack in the middle of my heart. It was the truth and it hurt. For years during his elementary school years (an extremely impressionable time in psychological development), his life was centered around basketball. There were games every weekend, and my large family attended in droves. Shaka's cousins, aunts, uncles, and grandparents would all attend, cheering him on and groaning in disappointment if he missed a shot. In addition to going to practice after school I forced him to practice at home, often admonishing him for not being committed enough to the game. I erroneously thought basketball was his choice, and I insisted on him giving it nothing less than one hundred percent. This was another example of me not recognizing my son's trauma, and as a parent I had the painful realization that I contributed to his trauma. Not intentionally but through minimizing the effect of his experiences on his self-esteem and self-concept.

I share this story because not only is it a good example of post-traumatic growth, but it is important to understand it doesn't have to be a seemingly tragic or traumatic event to negatively shape your self-concept, your beliefs, and cloud the colors you see. Trauma is highly subjective. If you perceived your event as traumatic to you then it was traumatic. Your perception of the event as traumatic is what matters and is the only requirement to determine trauma. Period. And it doesn't matter if others respond to the same event differently. My son had an adverse experience on the mall playground that day and every experience he had regarding his height attached itself to this experience. As we saw in an earlier chapter, it is not always the event but rather how an individual "experience" the event. Although I considered it trivial at the time, it is now clear to me that his experience at the mall playground had a profound effect on my son as a Black male. Had it been a singular experience it may have affected him differently, but this notion of him being too tall was continually reinforced throughout his entire childhood. He viewed every mention of his height as a negative affront that disregarded who he was, with his worth and value measured by others based on a physical trait.

I missed numerous opportunities to respond to my son's adverse experience because it did not fit into my package of what I considered trauma, and I was a trained therapist. As a result, I unintentionally exacerbated rather than mitigated the effect of this experience. The rugged burnt orange of the basketball was one of the colors he often saw his childhood through. But, again, because he was surrounded by a significant amount of pure, unconditional, real, and perfect love everywhere (PURPLE) it helped to assuage his negative experiences. I am grateful he has been able to turn his adverse experiences into art which has allowed him to see the world through a kaleidoscope of colors.

As an adult you may look at the world through the lens of a deeply ingrained (albeit faulty) belief system about yourself and life in general. Your lens may be so tainted that even when there is a rainbow of colors in your field of vision, you only focus on the brown. Just as there is an attachment to the new car, there is a powerful emotional attachment to your belief and your brain masterfully sees only that which it wants to see. Everything else fades into the background.

You may not have had the opportunity to transform your adverse experiences through an outlet such as art. The primary point is that there is PURPLE in your pain and there is a myriad of ways for it to manifest. Recognizing the value and the purpose of your painful experiences helps to transcend the pain and transform your lives.

Our painful experiences are part of what makes us who we are. It informs our character and helps to build our resilience. Scientific studies have shown that adults who have overcome childhood trauma are more resilient, more positive, and better able to handle challenges than adults who have not experienced or overcame traumatic adverse experiences.

My favorite Star Trek episode is the one where the Enterprise lands on a planet where the inhabitants did not experience any type of emotional pain or stress. I do not recall exactly, but there was something about the planet that wiped away all hurts, disappointments, and painful memories. The inhabitants walked around in a robotic-like state of imposed bliss. None of them demonstrated any character or personality as they moved about with perpetual smiles. Because anyone with feelings and painful memories was a threat to their blissful planet, the leaders of this world removed all of Captain Kirk's painful memories and infused him with joy and bliss so that he became robotic just like the other inhabitants. At some point, Captain Kirk realized that by giving up his painful memories, he no longer had a personality and there was nothing that was distinguishable between him and the other inhabitants. In a dramatic Captain Kirk flair, he theatrically declared "I need my pain." Truer words have never been spoken. Our painful experiences, all of them, make us who we are. They help to define our character and different nuances that make us individual.

Another good example is in the sitcom The Good Place, which is a comedy about the afterlife. As the series progresses over several seasons, the main characters are finally transported to the good place (i.e., nirvana, heaven, perpetual love and joy). In this good place one could have whatever they wanted simply by asking for it. There were no challenges, no struggles, no goals to work towards. Upon finally making it to this good place, they were disappointed to find the inhabitants to not only be zombie like, but they exhibited decreased brain capacity and mental function. In this place without challenges or problems to solve, there was no need for their cognitive abilities, and they began to lose the knowledge and intelligence they had developed during their lifetime on earth with its many challenges. In the beginning this idea of having anything they wanted was exciting and novel. But eventually they grew bored with the endless supply of whatever you want whenever you want it. And in this sense, the 'good place' had inadvertently turned out to be 'the bad place.'

Challenges and struggles are not just important to human evolution they are important to all living creatures. If the chick did not become uncomfortable in the egg, it would never go through the struggle of pecking its way out of the egg and it would never hatch. The same is true in the metamorphosis of the butterfly, it has to become uncomfortable in the caterpillar body that previously provided comfort.

There is a story of a kindhearted young boy intently watching a butterfly struggle in its attempt to emerge from its cocoon. As the little boy watched, he noticed that the butterfly was having a difficult time getting out of the cocoon and was only able to break small pieces of the cocoon at a time. The young boy's tender heart was touched by the apparent struggle, and he thought he would help the butterfly get free by breaking open the cocoon. So, he carefully peeled the rest of the cocoon from around the butterfly's body. Satisfied with what he felt was a kind act to help the butterfly, he expected to see it fly away free. But the newly released butterfly only laid on its side. As he looked closer, the boy noticed that the butterfly's wings were not fully formed. They seemed very frail and although the butterfly slowly moved them it was not able to fly. This made the little boy very sad, but what he did not know is that the struggle of breaking the cocoon is how the butterfly wings are strengthened for flight. In his effort to help the butterfly avoid its struggle and breaking open the cocoon, the little boy had rendered the butterfly flightless, limited to only crawling on the ground much like its former self, the caterpillar.

Pain is an inevitable part of the human experience as some challenges are necessary to develop strength and resiliency. Our painful experiences can become fodder for bitterness, anger, and resentments or they can be transformed into compassion, empathy, power, and love. Choose the latter.

I have used my personal trauma to guide my education and career choices. Because of the trauma I experienced I found passion and purpose in helping others to heal from their adverse experiences. It is not my role to take away another person's pain and challenges, rather to provide compassionate support as they find their own strength. Whether I am teaching, counseling, or coaching when I see the aha moment on someone's face – my pain has found purpose. The sexual, physical, emotional, and spiritual abuse I experience throughout my life; being abandoned by my father; and growing up in an angry and loveless environment – it all has purpose. I have chosen to use my pain to educate, empower, and motivate transformational healing in others. I wouldn't be who I am without the total sum of my experiences. Just as Captain Kirk made his declaration of needing his pain, if I could, I wouldn't change anything about my life. My past doesn't need to change -and neither does yours, only our relationship to our past needs to change. Afterall, I survived, and I now have a life filled with pure unconditional real and perfect love everywhere. While experiencing a crapload of childhood trauma is not a prerequisite to being a transformational healer, I know that my level of compassion, insight, strength, commitment, and passion wouldn't be the same without my personal experiences.

This is not an attempt to oversimplify the healing process. I did not go directly from acknowledging my trauma to healing others. I am an empath that is acutely sensitive to the emotions of others, and I have been this way my entire life. Long before I understood why I felt the pain of others and I was filled with compassion for others. As a child I and even now as an adult I am teased for being incredibly sensitive. Today I understand my sensitivity and I know that it is part of the inspiration and passion I have for helping others. But, the work of a transformational healer requires a strong life-long commitment to my personal healing process to do this work.

I believe personal experience is valuable, yet we cannot heal others from our pain. We can share empathy and compassion, but we can only empower others from a place of empowerment, and we can only heal others from our healing. Our pain allows us to resonate with the pain of others, which is why people that have experienced trauma tend to have a higher level of compassion than those that did not. But it is our healing that provides the insight for transformation. Doing transformational work with others has often exposed the unhealed and shadowy places within me. We cannot truly see ourselves except through the eyes of others. This is not always easy, and it can be painful when our trauma or the unhealed places in us are exposed. But because I am committed to my healing and growth, I recognize these exposures as a divine learning opportunity. I recognize that someone cannot push my button unless it is already installed. Whenever we are triggered by someone, it is calling forth something in us that needs healing. It is an opportunity to take a deeper dive and to do our own internal work. Just as other people's behavior and decisions may not reflect your truth, someone triggering you doesn't necessarily reflect their truth, as much as it mirrors something within us – often those parts of ourselves we would rather not see, the parts that need healing.

Once while facilitating a personal development workshop, there was a participant taking the course that immediately triggered me when she entered the room. I had never met this woman but as soon as she walked into the room I was triggered. Actually, she shuffled into the room crying and collapsed in her chair where she continued to weep. Now as a healer, I welcome and encourage tears, and I recognize the value they have to the healing process. But there was something victim like and attention seeking in her tears and body language. I immediately felt annoyed, and I am not proud of my response but rather than leaning in, I felt myself repelling from her. However, my next thought was, wow I wonder what button she has pushed inside me? I recognized that if I was being triggered it was because there was a button inside of me that was being pressed. So, I made a conscious decision to lean in and get curious about what would be revealed.

By the following afternoon much to my chagrin, rather than feeling compassion or connected, I was annoyed because I was even more triggered by her. This woman was deeply invested in her pain and the narrative of her story of trauma and abuse. She resisted all attempts to engage in the cognitive process of challenging her belief system. On the contrary, she would dig in harder if someone tried to offer suggestions to help her move through her pain. She could have been the poster child for the cognitive distortion 'inability to disconfirm'. No matter how much others tried to help her see a positive side, she resisted. I could sense the exasperation of the others in the room as they grew tired of giving her feedback only to have it rejected. As the workshop leader, I worked hard to maintain patience and compassion, but it was difficult.

At one point she decided this workshop, like everything else she had tried, wouldn't help her because of her deeply held belief that she was beyond help, and she got up and walked out. I instinctively followed her out of the room. It was the last day of the 3-day workshop, midafternoon with only a few hours left. I really did not think I would be able to get through to her, after all I had not been able to penetrate her shield the entire weekend. But I couldn't let her walk out without giving it another try.

In my professionally mastered neutral tone, I asked her what was going on and why she felt the need to leave. She began with her same litany of complaints: no one cares; no one understands her pain; she feels judged; she felt her needs were not being met; and no one wanted her there. Suddenly it clicked for me why I was so annoyed by her behavior. Her outside behavior triggered my inner posture, a posture that I worked hard to conceal from the world. My inner critic and faulty beliefs commanded that I did not act needy but, on the inside, I felt everything she was saying more than I would have admitted. I held a deep-seated belief that no one really understood me, no one wanted to be bothered, but I held a mandate that I must be strong and keep it together. I would not allow myself to sit in front of a group of people and act whiny and needy, but there was a part of me that felt alone and uncared for. And here she was holding up a mirror forcing me to acknowledge that part of myself that was needy and desperately wanted attention. She was acting the way I wanted to act at times, doing all the things I unlovingly derided myself for and that I wouldn't give myself permission to do. This was a deeply ingrained limiting belief because self-denial was probably my first protection and I had become a master at self-sufficiency.

In that moment, I realized it was not her that I was repelled by, but that part of myself where I still felt fear-based shame. The part of me that believed my needs wouldn't be met by others – so do not ask – and never let them know you are needy. As I shared earlier, I had a strong fear of being vulnerable. In spite of all the healing and transformational work I had done throughout the years, a part of me still felt I would be abandoned if dared ask for help. It was my subconscious belief I developed that I was a bother – that led me to become self-sufficient to a fault. And here this woman was triggering me and pushing the button where I had skillfully managed to hide my shame.

I suddenly felt a connection to the little girl in me that was still afraid of dying. The little girl whose muscles were still frozen and who still had a hard time breathing. This little girl was still terrified of being rejected, and afraid the world would discover she was an imposter and deem her as being unlovable. I felt a surge of compassion for that part of me that felt worthless, and in doing so, I suddenly felt my heart teeming with empathy and compassion for the woman standing in front of me holding up the proverbial mirror. The light that allowed me to see into my inner darkness, also allowed me to see her – to truly see her.

I do not remember what I said to her in that moment, and I know the words were not that important. I felt a genuine connection to her and whatever I said came from that place. There is a saying in the social service arena that "People don't care how much you know, until they know how much you care." This saying is absolutely true, especially for those that are hurt and/or wounded. Authenticity is key because their survival skills have taught them to look right through the bull crap. Whatever it was that I said was filled with more meaning for her because she was able to feel the genuine empathy and compassion that I was now feeling towards her. She felt seen and she felt understood, which made all the difference in the world for her. I was only able to see her because I was willing to see myself. I couldn't provide compassionate support from within the shadows. It was only when I was willing to expose my shadow to the light that I was able to express authentic compassion.

She returned to the workshop a different woman and was fully engaged for the next few hours. By the time the workshop ended she was literally transformed from the posture of a victim with limiting beliefs to an empowered woman with limitless potential. She wouldn't have gotten there if she had walked out. And she would have walked out if I had not been willing to journey into the darkness and face my own shame and pain. By no means am I taking credit for her transformation. The transformational work I do is not about fixing anyone. It is more about providing guidance, being a compassionate witness, and providing a safe space so that people can find the answer within themselves.

Self-awareness and self-acceptance are key to transforming your pain into your purpose. What strengths have you developed because of your painful experiences? Are you more resilient, more compassionate towards others? In what ways have you experienced post traumatic growth syndrome? What gifts or talents can you use to transfer your pain into purpose? Remember passion is borne out our pain and our passion is often the impetus for our purpose. What has brought you the most pain? What now brings you the most joy? What would you do tomorrow if money or skill were not an issue?

If you have a difficult time feeling passionate or imagining your purpose, spend some time free form writing using the prompts 'I am passionate about…' or 'My purpose is…' Don't filter your responses no matter how nonsensical they may be. It may take several writing sessions to figure it out, but do not give up. Them that seek PURPLE, shall find PURPLE. Look for the PURPLE, it is there within you and all around you waiting to be discovered.

We are not here to hide behind false evidence as it limits our potential. We all have a unique purpose, and just as no one else on the planet shares your fingerprint, no one shares your unique purpose. Even if you share the same occupation or talent – the space you occupy is uniquely yours. The people that will cross your path are unique to you. Whatever space you are in is changed because of your presence. Because of post-traumatic growth, I have experienced the gift of seemingly serendipitous interactions with clients and students that were pure magic. Many times, I have witnessed alchemic transformation, but it required both of us to be at that exact space, at that exact time. I have had many encounters that literally changed the trajectory of my life, and I wondered where I would be if those encounters with that specific person at that specific time had not happened.

I often think of the woman I spoke with when I called a suicide hotline with a lethal number of pills in my hand ready to take my life.

This stranger, that I had never met gave me just the glimmer of hope I needed to save my life. What pain had she experienced to give her the passion to help prevent suicide? I will never know, but what I do know is that her pain had purpose and this purpose was manifested the night she helped save my life. Prior to this fateful encounter I had been extremely suicidal with several hospitalizations for failed suicide attempts.

As far back as I can remember I thought of dying as a way out of my pain. My first actual suicide attempt happened when I was only ten years old. I don't recall the specific event that initiated the attempt, but I hated my life, my family, and myself and I just wanted to die. I felt no one cared about me because they constantly reminded me that I was too much of a bother, no one would care if I died. One of the verbal assaults my older brothers constantly assailed at me was "I wish you were dead." As a child without developed cognitive reasoning abilities my brain believed everyone would be better off if I was dead. To accomplish this task, I chewed a bottle of orange flavored baby aspirin, and in true Charlene dramatic flair, I strategically splayed myself on the hallway floor, with the bottle in my hand so that everyone could see me and feel bad about how mean they were to me. Clearly what I really wanted was attention. I wanted someone to recognize the pain I felt and to help me feel better. But what I got was my brothers literally stepping over me to tell my mother that I was being dramatic and acting crazy again.

Rather than displaying sympathy or compassion towards me, my mother yelled at me for eating the baby aspirin. In that moment I felt she was angrier that all of the baby aspirins were now gone, than she was that I wanted to die. She was not yelling because they could hurt me, she was yelling because now the bottle was empty, which translated in my brain to you really don't matter at all. She gave me this horrible tasting liquid that caused me to gag and throw up the baby aspirins, and nothing else was ever said. I do not know if it registered with her that the magnitude of my pain was so great that at ten years old, I was trying to kill myself. But there wasn't anything said about the suicide attempt and the emotional pain I felt was not addressed. This only left me feeling more dejected and I felt like the bottle of baby aspirins were more important to her. From that point on and even until this day I cannot tolerate the taste of anything orange flavored.

An unexpected consequence of that failed suicide attempt was that it actually helped me to deal with the pain and trauma of my life. The thought of suicide made my life bearable because I reasoned that if it got to be too unbearable, I could always just kill myself. It was my "in case of fire, break glass." I thought of it fondly and as a matter of fact, like someone would think of diet and exercise to lose weight. This gave me a sense of power over my life knowing I could end it anytime I wanted. Suicide is often described as a permanent solution to a temporary problem. As a child and a young adult, I did not have the cognitive ability to understand that my circumstances were temporary. I was blinded by the despair in my life, and I couldn't see any PURPLE.

As a survival mechanism, I started using drugs at the young age of eleven. Most people start using drugs out of curiosity or as a way to self-medicate. For me what started out as curiosity immediately became a form of self-medication to soothe the emotional pain. My introduction to mood- and mind-altering substances was marijuana, and it eased my emotional pain and made my home life bearable. And I desperately needed something to help me cope. I did not understand at the time what it meant to be an empath. All I knew was that I was constantly feeling my personal emotional pain or vibrating with the emotional pain of others. I was an extremely sensitive child living in a dangerous environment – raw and exposed. I was unable to mask myfeelings, and in my home, this was considered a weakness; therefore, I was constantly derided for being too sensitive or too dramatic. Drugs helped me ease the constant onslaught of feelings and to mask my emotions.

From the very beginning of my drug use, I used drugs like a fiend. I was wild, reckless and would try any drug that was offered to me without question and without any thought of possible consequences. The seventies were filled with all kinds of little pills, and I tried them all. Uppers, downers, and sideways. Surprisingly, I still did well in school when I decided to go because along with drugs, I started skipping classes to get drunk or high. Although I never did homework and I never studied I still managed to pass my classes. Once while in middle school, I skipped the entire day and showed up after school to cheerleading practice drunk. The coach cut me from the team and sent me home, not because I was obviously drunk, but because I had skipped school. The coach nor any other adult never said anything about me, who was only about thirteen years old, being totally inebriated. The seventies were a strange time.

As a young adult, the more my life raveled out of control with using harder more addictive drugs and toxic abusive relationships, the more suicide felt like a viable option. As a child I was suicidal because of how I was treated by others. But as an adult I was suicidal because of how I treated myself and allowed myself to be treated by others. I felt helpless and powerless, and I couldn't see any way out of the dark despair I constantly felt. I became obsessed with the idea of committing suicide as the only way out of my pain and I made several attempts and each time I was saved by divine intervention. I was hospitalized several times for suicidal ideations and/or attempts. Each time I was released from the psych ward, I would follow up by meeting with a therapist. These sessions were mandatory if I wanted to keep getting little happy pills they were prescribing.

I felt no connection to these individuals and would only attend one or two sessions. I did not have the language at the time, but I did not feel safe, and I would feel worse after leaving a session. At the time I had not shared my abusive childhood history with anyone. I had an incredible sense of shame around the things that happened in my childhood because I had long ago deduced that it was my fault they happened. These sessions were my first attempts to open up and start sharing but their response left me feeling judged or I felt they didn't believe some of the more horrific trauma. In the early eighties the field of psychology was still in its infancy. Trauma informed care was a language and a practice that did not exist. Even the vast array of psychotropic medications that we now have to treat depression and anxiety did not exist. Valiums, an early precursor to Xanax and other anti-anxiety medications, was considered the cure all, and it was doled out like candy. Mostly the therapists I saw during that time just seemed overwhelmed which only served to increase my shame. Therapy was scratched off my list as a way of helping, so I continued to use drugs and obsess about suicide.

Although I was suicidal, I still had a sense of vanity and pride, and I did not want to leave behind the legacy of suicide. It needed to look like a tragic accident. Thinking about ways to commit suicide and make it look like an accident occupied far too many of my thoughts. This actually saved my life on several occasions because although I was in hopeless despair, I would think – but I need a better plan. Once I was in my car ready to drive head on into a semi-truck, but was afraid to risk not dying, and ending up paralyzed. This was truly an extremely dark period in my life.

One of the most bizarre suicide attempts happened one night when I was filled exceedingly with the shame, self-loathing, and despair of an active addict that had been up three days without sleep. I felt the hopelessness and despair that had been my constant companion and I felt I couldn't face another day in this hell that was my life, so I enacted what I thought was the master plan. It was a cold night, by Florida standards, and I had been using a space heater to warm my bedroom. I turned on the space heater next to my bed, laid my pillow on top of the heater, and used my bedcovers to make a trail from the pillow to the bed. The idea was that it would appear I fell asleep and accidentally knocked the pillow on the heater, starting a house fire. In this plan, I would hopefully die from smoke inhalation so I wouldn't feel the pain of the fire, and everyone would feel sorry for the horrible way I died. End of my story. After swallowing a handful of pills that I had gotten from one of the doctors after my last suicide attempt, I drank a half bottle of liquor just to make sure I slept through the fire. This plan felt perfect and as the pills and booze took over, I closed my eyes and welcomed death.

Within a few hours or maybe it was only minutes, I woke up coughing to a strange smoky smell. At first, I thought I was dead but still smelled like smoke, but then I realized I was still in my bedroom, and to my disappointment, very much alive. Although the room was not on fire, there was a strange smoky smell that was making me cough. It was the incessant coughing that had woken me up out what I thought would be my final sleep. Dazed and confused, I looked on the floor towards the heater and discovered the pillow had not caught fire but had shrunk down to a little ball. What I soon realized is that it did not catch afire because as it turned out the pillow was flame retardant and rather than being kindling to start the house fire, the pillow just melted from the heat. Years later I laughed and joked about this suicide attempt, but it was not a laughing matter at the time and suicide never is. I was emotionally and spiritually destitute. I couldn't see beyond the pain, and I was seeking a permanent solution to what was a temporary problem.

I have so much compassion and my heart aches for the person I was and for anyone else who felt so much emotional pain that suicide seemed a viable option. What I know now that I didn't know then, is that my pain was attached to a purpose that was alive inside me the entire time. I had so very much to live for, but I couldn't see it at the time because I only saw the brown in my life. Today when I hear of someone committing or attempting suicide my heart aches because while I understand the kind of pain that drives someone to take their own life, I also know what is on the other side of that pain. I know that healing happens, and that our lives can be transformed from the inside out. Pain is temporary but suicide is permanent. It breaks my heart that so many people will never know the joy of moving beyond the pain and realizing the PURPLE in their midst.

My last suicide attempt, the one where I called the suicide hotline, happened right before I entered residential treatment for my drug addiction. Clearly my life was out of control because no one volunteers for residential drug treatment unless all other options had failed. Through a miraculous course of events, I found a women's treatment program in Boston that agreed to accept me into their program. I had flown from Florida to Boston where I was interviewed at the program on a Friday. I was accepted into the program, but because they did not accept new clients into the program on Fridays, I had to wait until Monday to enter. The woman that interviewed me asked if I had a safe place to stay until Monday and reminded me, I needed to stay clean until then. There was an older man that I had been manipulating for money who lived right outside Boston. He had purchased my airline ticket to Boston, and I would stay with him until Monday.

110

I was genuinely grateful and relieved that I had been accepted into the program and I had every intention of not using drugs and staying clean until Monday. But I had no control over my addiction, it was as though I was possessed. Friday night I went to bed early but all-day Saturday I was anxious, struggling with what felt like a monster inside of me. I lost the battle and by Saturday night, I had taken all the money out of the man's wallet, and I took his car without permission while he was in the bathroom. I was in a strange city, where I didn't know anyone, and I was not familiar with the neighborhoods. But there I was out like a fiend hunting down drugs. The insanity of that night alone could be an entire book, but to sum it up I was involved in a high-speed chase after I gave a stranger money for drugs, and he took off in a car. Foolishly, I took off after the car and a high-speed chase ensued. In my insane pursuit of this vehicle, I wrecked the vehicle twice. This man helped me get to Boston and allowed me to stay at his home, I repaid him by stealing his money and wrecking his car.

I finally gave up and went in search of more drugs in a vehicle that was barely drivable. At this point in my addiction, I was an intravenous drug user, not only did I need to buy drugs I needed to also procure the works (as the needle was called). I bought a used needle from a stranger on the streets without much of a second thought. It was the mid-eighties and AIDS had recently been discovered and IV drug use was one of the leading means of infection. That needle itself could have been a death sentence and I am eternally grateful I escaped my addiction without contracting HIV, but at the time I did not care.

After copping drugs (again from a stranger on the street) I went in search of the nearest public restroom that I could use to shoot the dope into my veins. I ended up getting high inside of a Kentucky Fried Chicken bathroom. There was only one bathroom in the place, and it was in the kitchen area where food was being prepared. It was a single stall and people kept knocking on the door, but I couldn't stop. I was trying to shoot all the drugs I had copped into my veins. I was in there so long that the staff started banging on the door and threatened to call the police. I finally came out sweating, wild eyed, with blood running down my arm and on my clothes. I will never forget the horror and disgust on the faces of the employees and the customers as I finally walked out of that bathroom with blood still streaming down my arm. Through the glaze of the drugs, I saw them back up and move out of my path. I could see them watching out the window as I got into the twice wrecked, banged-up car with the bumper dragging on the ground and pulled off.

I too was horrified by my behavior, and I literally hated myself. I did not want to be out using drugs like an out-of-control fiend, locked in a dirty Kentucky Fried Chicken bathroom unable to stop sticking that needle into my arm. But I had no control. I felt as though I was the worse human being on the planet, and I just wanted to die. I looked forward to getting back and taking the pills I had stashed. And this time I knew there were enough pills so that I could finally go to sleep and never wake up again. I knew that I couldn't do this ever again and if death was the only way out – so be it. What I did not know at the time was this really would be my last time getting high. The date was August 16, 1986.

I returned to the house of my transgressions because I had nowhere else to go. My arrival was noisily announced by the pieces of the wrecked car that was dragging on the ground. At this point I did not have any fight left in me and I knew that I was done. I had never done anything like this, and I was at an all-time low. All that I was thinking was I could not wait to die and end it all. I expected him to call the police and have me arrested, but my plan was to commit suicide before the police arrived. The reaction I received from him only confused me more. Rather than the anger or even the police I expected, I was met first with relief that I was alive, and then shock at the condition of me and the car. This was followed by what I could only interpret as pity and disdain as he moved away from me much in the same manner as those at the Kentucky Fried Chicken.

I was done with trying to fight the losing battle against my addiction and I surrendered. Once I got inside, I pulled out my stash of suicide pills that I kept for such a time as this, and there was enough of them to kill a horse. Because I had attempted suicide by taking pills and I survived, I would make sure I did not survive this. I was crying while looking at them in my hand, and I realized that I no longer cared if people knew I committed suicide. In fact, I wanted everyone to know how miserable my life was. Even then I knew there were people that cared about me. My sister Gwen, my grandmother, and even my mother had changed and was trying to show me she cared. But I didn't care enough about myself, and I was tired of disappointing those that did care about me.

There was something different about this suicide attempt. I felt a kind of resolve – a surrender to my death. This time I was not concerned with whether other people cared about me. I realized that all this time I had been blaming others for not caring about me, but I did not care about me. In fact, I loathed and hated myself because of my behavior and the choices I had made because of my addiction. I had the opportunity to come to Boston for treatment and to change my life. But here I was within one day at an all-time low and a bottom I never imagined.

Prior to this attempt, I had tried several times to stop using drugs. Once I tried to stop by returning to the church of my youth, and I quickly became a judgmental religious zealot. I didn't do any work to address my childhood trauma and other underlying issues because I felt God had magically cured me of my addiction. I was only on my high horse a few months when an ex-boyfriend came by to have bible study with me and just happened to leave a bag of cocaine on my bathroom counter. I came crashing down off that high horse and all my religion went out the window. So much for the magic cure.

Once after an overdose that landed me in the hospital, I entered residential treatment, but within a few months I memorized the literature and managed to convince the counselors that I was ready to be transitioned to outpatient treatment. Within days of leaving residential treatment, I was shooting cocaine into my veins in the bathroom of the outpatient program and still had the audacity to walk into the group and try to pretend I wasn't high as a sat there with a puddle of sweat forming around me.

After all these failed attempts, I felt helpless and hopeless. The previous events of the evening convinced me that my addiction was all-consuming and far too powerful and I would never be able to stop. I did not want to live as an active addict another day. I felt a despair so deep and an unworthiness so great I couldn't see any other way out of my misery.

I had never done this in the past, but for some reason (clearly a divine power) I felt the need to explain to someone why I was committing suicide, so I called a suicide hotline. This was one of the things they drilled in the therapy sessions I attended after my suicide attempts, but I always considered a suicide hotline an oxymoron. I had wondered at the time why would someone call a hotline if they are seriously trying to kill themselves? But clearly a seed was planted because I called the hotline. At the time I made the call I did not think it would help me, nor was that my purpose for making the phone call. I called because I was too ashamed to call anyone else and I wanted someone to know the exact reason for my suicide. I wanted them to know that I really was very sorry, but I had no choice because I couldn't continue to live as an addict controlled by my addiction. Unlike my other suicide attempts in the past where I felt more anger and revengeful than I did remorseful, this time I was filled with deep sorrow and couldn't stop crying. But, again, I felt I had no choice and I needed to go through with the plan, and this call would serve as my suicide letter.

I called the hotline and as soon as the woman answered my sobbing increased. The woman on the other end of the line talked to me and listened to me as a I cried about how much I hated myself and my life and why death felt like the only option. I told her I was supposed to go in treatment on Monday but did not think I could make it after what I had done that night. I explained to her that I felt so much shame and that I did not want to live another day. She prayed with me and encouraged me to hold on one more day and go into treatment and she assured me that my life would get better. She was compassionate and said she understood that I must be in a lot of pain and that she knew how desperately I wanted the pain to stop.

If there was any one thing in this conversation that was paradigm shifting was her validation of my pain and my emotions. Her voice was comforting as she assured me treatment would help me learn to deal with my pain and that I would have a second chance at life. Her words, her prayer, and her compassion was enough in that moment, to give me just a flicker of hope. She convinced me to flush the pills down the toilet and she spoke with the man whom I had stolen from and wrecked his car. I am not sure what she said to him, but she stayed on the phone while he witnessed me flushing the pills down the toilet. I now recognize that I needed to die that night, not physically but metaphorically, so that a new me could be reborn. This woman helped me to get to the other side of my desperate despair.

I do not know that woman's name or anything else about her. She doesn't know me and may never know the profound affect her words had in changing the course of my life. I do not know if there would have been a different outcome if someone else had answered the phone. I do not know what personal trauma and pain she had suffered to birth the passion to help prevent suicide. But what I do know is her purpose manifested that night in my life. If she never helped anyone else, her helping me that night and it changed the entire trajectory of my life with an incalculable ripple effect, not only in my life and the life of my loved ones but on my future life and everyone I would interact with in the future. I now realize that there would have been a huge hole in the world that I should have been occupying and I am incredibly grateful for this nameless woman for helping to save my life.

I entered treatment on Monday and my life has never been the same. In recovery I was able to go to college and chose an academic and career path that allowed me to help hurting women and others affected by drug addiction and trauma. I know I have had pivotal transformational moments with hundreds, maybe thousands of individuals. However, I am very clear that none of that would have happened had I not reached out to that hotline because there was no doubt that those pills would have killed me. On August 16,1986 had not that faceless women answered that suicide hotline with the perfect temperament and the perfect words at the perfect time I wouldn't have made it to Sunday. I would have died in my sea of brown, and I would have never experienced the transformation of my pain to passion that filled my life with purpose and PURPLE.

Our presence on the planet affects an unimaginable number of people and circumstances. I have worked with men and women in residential treatment program who loss or were in the process of losing custody of their children. Most of these individuals were involved in the criminal justice system. The statistics are very clear, that if a child has a parent involved in the criminal justice system that child has a seventy-percent chance of becoming involved in the system as well. The parents' recovery literally changes the trajectory of their children's life and their children's children for generations to come. When you help one person or offer a kind word you may never know the ripple effect.

Your purpose doesn't have to be found in your occupation. Sometimes it is as simple as smiling and saying hello to a stranger or holding space and listening to a friend that could literally makes all the difference in the world. I cannot tell you what your purpose is. But I can tell you that healing your pain and your relationship with yourself will awaken you to your potential, which will ignite your passion. Your purpose can always be found in your passions and amongst the beautiful colors of the rainbow when you look for the PURPLE.

The following exercise provides an opportunity to discover your passion and your purpose and to take steps towards manifesting your dreams. Dream big and then take baby steps. Maybe you cannot eradicate world hunger, but you could support your local food bank or serve meals to the homeless. I have a nephew that fills sandwich bags with snacks such as peanut butter crackers or granola bars. He hands these snacks out to the homeless individuals that congregate in certain parts of the city. Sure, they are only snacks, but in his offer, he is saying to them you matter to me. Someone could be at the end of their rope, but the snacks and a kind word from my nephew could make the difference between life or death for a homeless person. We might want to save the world, but what we do for individuals in our own community makes all the difference in the world.

Use the columns below to respond to the following. A word of encouragement: Please do not attempt to censor what you write. Fear and faulty beliefs may manifest by convincing you to dream small to remain in the safety of playing small. But if your dreams and goals are not a little scary, you are dreaming too small. Confront your fears

> If your dreams and goals are not a little scary, you are dreaming to small.

and faulty beliefs by writing down your biggest dreams. After all they are only words on paper – at least for now.

Column 1 – What would you do if money, education, time, or fear were not a barrier? What type of work would you do without being paid if money were not an issue? Where would you live if you could live anywhere in the world? How would you make a difference in the world if you had access to unlimited resources?

Column 2 – Spend some time thinking about what you wrote in column 1. Why is this important to you? What are your personal values? What value does it bring to others? Responding to these questions provides insight into what you are passionate about.

Column 3 – What baby steps can you begin to take right now? What goals would you need to accomplish to manifest the dreams you identified in column 1? The goals should be s.m.a.r.t. goals (specific, measurable, attainable relevant, and time bound).

Column 4 – What steps/actions can you take now to begin the process of manifesting your dreams? These could be mini/daily goals such as google the requirements for the occupation you are interested in. Perhaps you could begin volunteering at a community organization that provides the services that you are passionate about.

Column 1	Column 2	Column 3	Column 4
What are your dreams? What would you do if there were no barrier?	Why is this important? What is the value of your dream?	What goals would you need to accomplish? Are they realistic?	What steps can you take now to begin manifesting your goals & dreams.

Chapter Seven

Beyond Your Wildest Dreams

On a beautiful Monday morning, late in the summer of 1986, I entered residential treatment at Women, Inc. in Boston, Massachusetts. My intake was with Joy, the same woman that interviewed me on the previous Friday. The irony of her name was not lost on me. Joy was sharp, fierce, and beautiful. With her light-brown complexion and short wavy hair, she was dressed to the nine in slacks and a button-down shirt, and she exuded the confidence of a woman that was used to being admired. I immediately felt intimidated by her. I learned early to use my charm and flattery as a tool whenever I was trying to manipulate a situation to my advantage, and it did not matter if it was male or female. I was feeling so uncomfortable, afraid, alone, and I wanted her to like me and to consider me worthy of entering this program. I did what came natural for me and started batting my eyelashes and turning up my lip in what I hoped was a subtle seductive overture. Obviously, it was not that subtle because she looked at me like I had just grown two extra heads. Her piercing eyes looked directly into mine as if to say do not even try it. I felt that she saw every horrible thing about me, and I was suddenly so consumed by shame that my face started itching. I averted my eyes and wished I could vaporize into thin air. My limiting beliefs were running roughshod in my brain. I was not wanted there I was not worthy of treatment. I was too much of a dope fiend to ever stop using. What was I thinking about going to Boston for treatment, away from everything familiar? I felt I had made a horrible mistake. I wanted to get up, run out the door, get on a plane, and go home.

Just as I was thinking I should just get up and leave, a woman appeared at the door and stood silently until Joy looked up from the paperwork she was completing and acknowledged her with a slight nod. Joy then said to me "this is your big sister Janice (not her real name). You will shadow her for the next few days. She will show you the ropes and teach you the rules of the program." So much for my plan to walk out. I couldn't leave then because I would have to get past the woman in the doorway and I immediately felt intimidated by her no-nonsense demeanor. I decided to stay until I could make other arrangements. I watched as Joy and Janice searched through all my belongings including all pockets, the lining of my suitcase, and even the lining of my shoes. It had never occurred to me to bring drugs or contraband into the treatment program, and I was highly offended by the invasiveness of the search. Who did they think I was? Then I quickly remembered I was checking into a drug treatment center.

After the humiliating search, I was escorted upstairs by Janice to a large bedroom with four single beds. Janice informed me this was my room and instructed me to put my clothes down and get a change of clothes for the shower. "The shower?" I asked incredulously. "Yes, the shower", she said. "They don't let anyone in here without a shower first, women come here right from the streets." I wanted to say that I did not come from the streets and that I had just showered that morning, but instead, I obediently followed her down the hall to a communal bathroom with three shower stalls.

The house was an old New England Victorian mansion that was probably built in the 1800's and it had certainly seen better days. There was thick plastic covering a missing window and the walls needed a fresh coat of paint. But every corner of that house was clean. It smelled of pine cleanser and the wooden floors shined with decades of built-up wax. The bathroom, aside from a rusty radiator, was spotless. Janice told me to strip down and step into the shower. She watched me like a correction officer as I shamefully removed my clothing and stepped into the shower. She then poured some type of medicated shampoo into my hand and instructed me to rub it into the hair on my head and my pubic area. I hesitated and she told me that the shampoo would kill lice, crabs, or any other creature that was crawling around on me. She laughed at her attempt at humor, but I did not find it funny. Not at all. Again, I felt offended by the invasiveness of it all as she literally watched me rub in the shampoo as instructed. I felt humiliated or maybe in was the beginning of feeling humbled, something that I would learn a lot about over the course of my treatment at Women, Inc.

She noticed my distress as my eyes filled with tears and a few slid down my cheeks and she attempted to comfort me by sharing about herself and the program. "This is great program, if you really want help, you are in the right place. But, and she paused here for emphasis, 'It is hard though. Most women don't make it, they end up leaving because it's too hard. Those women aren't ready to give up the dope. You got to be ready to give it all up if you want to beat the dope. I've been here for three months, me and my baby. My son is eleven months old, and he lives here with me. No other program would let me bring him into treatment with me. I didn't want to leave my baby and I couldn't stop using, but I would have died if I had to be separated from my baby. He is downstairs in the daycare right now with the other kids that live here. This program is giving me a chance to be a mother to him. I wasn't a mother to my other children because the dope had me strung out. Staff is hard and strict but that is because they care, and they want us to beat the dope."

She carried on and on, while I showered and panicked internally. The dope? Why does she keep referring to the dope like it is an entity unto itself? Staff is strict and hard. Babies, children? They did not say anything about babies and children when I came for my interview. I liked kids but a treatment program with children, I did not sign up for this. As soon as I could I needed to figure out how to get back to Florida.

"Are you ready to give up the dope?" It felt more like a challenge than a question. She was looking right in my eyes. I had a quick flash of my last night using and I quickly averted my eyes because I was overcome with a sense of shame, and I felt less than dirt. I mumbled "I guess so". She practically yelled, "you got to more than guess so if you want to make it here, you got to know that you know that you are ready to give up the dope." She went on, "I want you to make it. All my other little sisters left. The dope was calling them, and they gave up. They wanted the dope more than they wanted to stay clean. I don't want you to give up. You came here all the way from Florida, you must want this pretty bad. You can't give up."

Janice was intense, but there was something likable about her. I could sense that beneath her veneer, she was a caring person. She was explaining that for the first few weeks I wouldn't be allowed to go anywhere in the house by myself and I would be chaperoned by another client everywhere I went including the bathroom, until I earned the trust of the group. She was still talking but more calmly now. It was as though she was reading my mind when she said, "You don't have to feel ashamed here. We have all done horrible things for the dope. But they teach us we are not horrible people, we never have to use dope again, and we can live a life beyond our wildest dreams." For the first time in a very long time, I felt something in me that was akin to optimism and thought there might be hope for me after all.

After I showered and dressed, all under Janice's watchful eye, and she then escorted me back downstairs and into a large room where about twelve women of every age and race sat around a huge table that was a hodgepodge of folding tables and dining tables pushed together. I sat down at the table next to Janice, and one of the first things I noticed after scanning the faces of the women was a handmade poster on the wall directly in front of me that read "Beyond Your Wildest Dreams". There it was again. How ironic I thought wearily because I think I must be in a nightmare.

An older Black woman with a short gray afro was speaking when I walked in and sat down. I was too busy taking in my surroundings to really listen to what she was saying, But when she angrily slammed her fist on the table, she got my full attention. "I am sick and tired of the dope lying to me" she screamed. She went on shouting, "It keeps telling me to leave the program, saying it will be different this time. I'm scared because I can only remember the good times." Several women began to prompt her with questions such as "what have you lost because of the dope?" "Are you allowed to see your grandchildren?" "Do you have a home to go to if you leave?" "Who cares about you on the streets?" They were bombarding her with questions. Some of the women were shouting the dope is a liar. It's trying to trick you so it can kill you?" I was overwhelmed by what felt like utter chaos. I was looking around frantically, wondering where staff was when suddenly the older woman jumped to her feet with her hands raised as though she had just won a championship fight. She yelled "The dope is a liar. I refuse to listen to it any longer. I am not leaving treatment. I'm fighting for my life. I am going to stay here until I get my life together and the dope can kiss my ass." The other women around the table began to clap and cheer. Some jumped up and gave her hugs. I felt like I had witnessed some sort of exorcism, and I decided right then that as soon as I could speak with my mother I would ask her to send me a plane ticket so I could get the hell out of this place.

When they all calmed down, Janice made the announcement "I have a new little sister. Her name is Charlene, and she is from Florida. Please introduce yourselves to her." I felt her sense of pride in me, and it helped to bolster my faltering self-esteem. The women sitting around the table dutifully began to introduce themselves. Just as Janice did earlier most of them declared how hard the program was, but all followed up with they were glad to be in a place where staff genuinely cared. It was all so overwhelming that I started to tune them out as I stared at the places where the tables were pushed together. This focus was providing an anchor for me and helped me to stay in my seat when everything in me wanted to get up and run right out the door.

Entering this program in Boston had already taken a multitude of miracles, serendipities, and divine interventions. As my life began to flash before my eyes, I was acutely aware that my entire life had been filled with divine interventions, synchronicities, and miracles. I grew up feeling unwanted, unloved and the classic family scapegoat, and I ran away from home shortly after turning seventeen. With only four months left of my senior year I dropped out of high school and ran off to be with the love of my life. I had fallen head over hell (pun intended) for who I thought was the man of my dreams. He was twenty-four-years-old with slick black hair, stunningly handsome with chiseled features, and a smile that made my heart skip beats. I loved everything about him – his walk, his talk, his clothes, his laugh. He doted on me, paid attention when I talked, and showered me with affection and gifts. I shared about some of the physical and verbal abuse I experienced at home, and he comforted me by assuring me that my family did not care about me. He promised he would always love and cherish me. He seemed too good to be true, and he was.

As it turned out, I was not his only girlfriend. There were glaring signs everywhere, but I was so naive, I ignored all warning signs and never questioned him. After all, he was a sophisticated worldly man, and I was still in high school. He never took me to his house, and I assumed he lived with someone, but I was convinced he was in love with me and with my faulty belief system, that was all that mattered. I fantasized that once I finished high school, we would get a place together and live happily ever after. His girlfriend was from the same neighborhood. I didn't know her because she was older, but I knew about her family because all the girls in that family had a bad reputation of being loose and streetwise.

It all came to a head when the mother of his girlfriend found out that he was dating me, and that I was underage and still in high school. She went to my mother and told her that he was a dangerous and abusive man. She described to my mother how he physically and mentally abused her daughter and kept her away from her family including her children. She informed my mother that she was raising her daughter's two kids because she was brainwashed and chose to be with him rather than her kids. She told my mother that he was responsible for getting her daughter strung out on drugs

Coincidentally, the same night his girlfriend's mother went and spoke to my mother, I had gotten particularly bold and stayed out all night at a hotel with Mr. Love of My Life. The next morning when he was bringing me home, we turned on my street and saw a police car at my house and we both panicked. I was only seventeen and he was twenty-four. I was under-age jailbait, and he could go to jail. There was no way I was going to let that happen. So, we rode around for a while and after the police left, he dropped me off a few blocks from my house. As soon as I walked into the house, my mother physically attacked me with an extension cord (her weapon of choice) and confronted me with the information about Mr. Love of My Life. She forbade me from ever seeing him again. She threatened to call the police and have him arrested because I was still a minor. But I did not feel like a child. In my mind I was a grown woman in love with a grown man. I felt my mother was the evilest person alive and that she was just trying to keep me away from him because she did not want me to be happy and he made me happy. I did not believe he was abusive or any of the horrible things she said about him. She said he used and abused women, but I did not believe her. I knew he did not have a regular job and I never questioned where the money came from that he constantly spent on me. He was always dressed nicely and driving nice cars. He told me he worked for a rentalcar company, which explained why he was always driving different brand-new cars. I bought the lie and did not question any of the glaring inconsistencies. This relationship was an extension of my relationships with my mother and my brothers, and I had learned early to deny my feelings, thoughts, and needs. I was so desperate to be loved, and I wanted to be part of his world at any cost.

When I was with him, I felt beautiful and the way he treated me made me feel special. I did not believe he could be abusive. This man was gorgeous, and I thought he could have any woman he wanted, and he had chosen me. I was not going to give him up and I did not care if he had another girlfriend. I didn't believe he could care about her the way he cared about me. My self-worth was so low, and my faulty beliefs about love and relationships were so skewed, I was willing to accept crumbs as long as I was at the table. Besides, I believed that he loved me, and I believed that my mother did not. The choice was easy. That night, with my younger sister Gwen crying and begging me not to leave, I climbed out my bedroom window carrying only what I could fit into a brown paper bag. I was going to be with my man, and I did not care what my mother or anyone else thought about him.

I thought I was running away from abuse and lovelessness to the arms of love except Mr. Love of my Life turned out to be Mr. Evil of my Life. He was very controlling, but in the beginning, I confused his control for love. I was operating at such a deficit that I couldn't differentiate love from abuse. He chose my clothes and told me what to wear and I willingly let him. He instructed me as though I was a child on how to sit and even how to eat my food. He had this weird thing against finger foods and even pizza had to be eaten with a knife and fork. At first, I relished his control. I thought of him as smart and worldly and felt he was grooming me to be a sophisticated woman, so I willingly complied with all his requests.

He stopped trying to hide other women from me. There were times he would take me with him and leave me in the car while he went inside to change clothes or pick something up. Some of the women we hung around worked in strip clubs and I was so desperate to get this man's love and for him to see me as a woman that I told him that I wanted to started dancing at a club. At first, he discouraged me, not because he cared so much about me, but because I was still only seventeen and we were basically in hiding from my family. We moved around between cheap hotels and furnished rooms. A few times we went out of state, and I worked in strip clubs in strange towns. At seventeen my most recent job had been working at Disney World. I was blown away by how much money I could make in one weekend dancing in those clubs. I detested the creepy men that came into those clubs, but I pretended to like them and found I had a knack for lying and running game and I told them whatever I thought they wanted to hear. Although he didn't ask for it, I gave all my money to Mr. Evil. After all, I reasoned that he was the one paying all the bills and buying me clothes, food, and drugs. We stayed in fancier hotels and furnished rooms. I was with the love of my life, and I thought I was in heaven. Little did I know, the road I was traveling was a slippery slope to hell.

It took a few months before the physical abuse started, but once it did, he turned out to be more abusive physically, emotionally, and verbally than I could ever have imagined. But because I ran away from home to be with him, I believed my fate was sealed and that I had no other choice except to stay with him. I felt my family was angry and ashamed of me and I had nowhere else to go. He was extremely controlling and forbade me from talking to my mother or anyone in my family because he was worried that they would call the police on him because I was still only 17 years old.

Mine was a classic textbook case for an abused woman. I made excuses for his behavior while working constantly to appease him, monitoring his moods and my one goal in life became to please him so he would not get angry. And just like a classic textbook case of an abusive man he was always contrite after the physical abuse and showered me with affection – until the next time. And those next times started getting closer and closer together and he became more and more unpredictable to the point that anything would trigger him. I wasn't talking enough, I was talking too much, I was dressed too nice, or I was not dressed nice enough. I smiled too much when I was talking to his friends, or I was not friendly enough. It took me a long time to figure out that my behavior had nothing to do with his wild mood swings. Not only did this man have serious mental health issues, but he was also addicted to heroin. He had shared with me early in our relationship that he had been diagnosed with mental health issues while in the Navy and received a medical discharge. I was too naive to understand what that meant as it related to his behavior. He had made it seemed like he faked the mental illness to get out of the navy. He didn't seem mentally ill, so I believed him. And it took me over a year to figure out the relationship between his behavior and the drugs. Because he wasn't an IV drug user and only snorted heroin, I didn't think he could be addicted like some of the junkies I had seen, because he did not use needles, I was so gullible.

I too was using a lot of drugs because I couldn't work in those clubs without them. I started snorting heroin with him and I was so naïve that the first time I got dope sick I didn't even know what was happening. I thought I had the flu but one of the women at the club told me I was dope sick and I couldn't believe it. There was no way I could be a junkie if I did not use needles. But to my surprise, as soon as I snorted some heroin all symptoms ceased. This woman told me that if I didn't want to get strung out that I shouldn't use it more than three days in a row. I played this mind game for a while, but I used some type of drug every day to cope with the hell that had become my life.

All the money I was making we never got a permanent place to live because that money was spent as fast as it came in. It seemed I was the only one making money because all he did now was lounge around or drive around all day in the car I had bought. I was terrified of him and afraid that if I left him, he would carry out his threat to kill me. A few times I did get the courage to leave, until he would find me and convince me that he loved me and couldn't live without me – my faulty beliefs that I was unworthy and unlovable led me to choose him over and over. I felt such shame and self-loathing at my inability to stay away from him, which validated my belief that I was unworthy and unlovable. I was in a perpetual vicious circle spinning out of control in a whirlwind of brown.

I was arrested several times for petty crimes I committed for Mr. Love of My Life (or so I thought). I was in such denial, continuously lying to myself that I could make him return to the man I fell in love with. Finally, we both got arrested because as it turned out I had unwittingly been part of a ring that was cashing forged refund checks at Sears Department store. One of the women that worked at the store was in in cahoots with Mr. Evil. I had no idea, and I used my real identification to cash the checks that she printed in my name for some alleged return he had made when he conveniently forgot his driver's license.

I was terrified because I had never committed a felony, I was not a criminal, and I was afraid of going to jail or prison. The Public Defender assigned to me suggested that since I had never had a felony charge that the judge might go easy on me, if he saw I was trying to better myself and get away from the criminal environment. He suggested that before my hearing came up that I enroll in school to get my GED, take a trade so that I could do something productive with my life. Out of fear of going to prison I enrolled at the local vocational school where I discovered that I had already earned enough credits to graduate when I dropped out high school and I was able to get my high school diploma.

I enrolled in clerical classes because, in the seventies, every woman I knew aspired to become a secretary. It was a good, respectable job and I wanted to be good and respected. While in school I began to catch glimpses of my true self. I realized I loved learning, and I felt alive for the first time in years. School gave me confidence and a hope for a decent future. I ended up only receiving two years of probation, and Mr. Evil was sentenced to prison. After spending years accepting horrific abuse, I was finally free.

I aced secretarial school, and I landed a job at a downtown law firm as a legal secretary. But there is a saying in the 12 Step program that neglected issues do not die, they have babies. I was fixing up the outside, but I had not done any work to heal my trauma or change my limiting beliefs and my issues were having babies. The man that would eventually become my husband (twice) turned me on to free basing cocaine and my drug use got out of control. No longer limited to partying on the weekends, I started using cocaine daily. I would wake up with every intention of going to work and convince myself of the same lie every day "I'm going to just do a little bit to get my day started.' Another saying from the 12-Step program – one is too many and a thousand is not enough. A few hours would pass and before I knew it, it was noon time. Sometimes I called in with some crazy excuse, sometimes I felt too ashamed to call. It just so happened that the attorney I worked for was a recovering alcoholic heavily involved in Alcoholic Anonymous. It was clear to him I had a problem with drugs. There were times I would leave for lunch and not make it back to work. He really tried to work with me because when I was good, I was very good at my job, but he eventually had to let me go after giving me some fatherly advice to get help. I promptly ignored his advice.

Without the responsibility of the job my addiction spiraled out of control. My life became a series of three-day binges followed by deep self-loathing shame and regret. People often think that addicts are choosing their lifestyle because they erroneously think that addiction is the easy way out. Nothing could be further from the truth. Addiction is hard, in fact it is by far the hardest thing I ever done – other than getting clean. I hated the drugs, I hated the power they had over me, and I hated the way I felt when I used. I hated being up all night unable to sleep listening to the birds as they started to chirp with the sunrise and the cars starting as my neighbors went to work. I hated not being able to hold down a job, pay my bills, spend time with family and friends, or keep my commitments. I hated it all. I swore every day I was going to stop, but I was unable to stop – my brain was hijacked. The drugs dominated my brain and was its major drive, coming before food, sex, or human connection.

One of the primary characteristics of addiction is the inability to stop using drugs despite negative consequences. I experienced the loss of jobs, relationships, and self-respect but still I was unable to stop. And

I wanted to stop, I really wanted to stop because I was miserable. Every day I would promise myself, God, and anyone who listened that I was done, and I was not going to do it again. I did not have any information on addiction, and I did not understand its nature. I felt insane and I honestly felt as though I was possessed. I felt a demonic spirit would take over my mind and I was helplessly at its mercy. I told my mother that I felt possessed and that I believed someone had put a hex on me. Growing up in Florida we were taught to believe in God, but we were also taught to believe in the power of the root man. When folk were having a string of bad luck, rather than look at their own behavior for the cause of such luck they made statements such as "the devil is busy" or "somebody put roots on me." My mother was a strong believer in both schools of thought, and she told me to be ready at 3 AM because she was going to take me to see someone who could break any demonic hex or spell.

We rode for hours in the early morning dark and stopped when we were deep in the woods of North Florida. Arriving pre-dawn, I was shocked to see the number of people that were already there, sitting around in the huge yard, both utterly desperate and hopeful at the same time. I saw the mother of one of my old high school boyfriends and his sister there, making the whole scene feel more like a dream than reality. After waiting hours, I met with the root conjurer who had a reputation of being the most powerful one in Florida and told him about my inability to stop using drugs even though they were ruining my life. He gave me some brightly colored and fragrant rocks and instructed me to sprinkle some in front of my door and to burn some in my house. He guaranteed that it would keep the demonic spirit away from me and my home. I went home hoping the spell would work and that I would finally be free of the bondage of using drugs. I dutifully placed some of the rocks outside my front door and placed some in an ashtray and lighted them with a match. The rocks started to crackle and pop, much like the crackle and pop of rock cocaine, and within seconds of burning the rocks I was triggered by the smell because it smelled like the free-base cocaine I was addicted to smoking. Of all senses, the olfactory, or smell, nerves have the most direct access to the memories and emotions stored in our brains, which is why we can be transported back to our grandmother's kitchen where it was safe and warm by the smell of a baking cake, or on the flip side, if you had an abusive father, the smell of the aftershave he wore when you were a kid could trigger a fear response. I was so triggered by those burning rocks that I had an overwhelming craving for rock cocaine. I immediately left my house leaving the rocks burning, while I headed straight for the Base House, which was the place that both sold drugs and allowed people to sit around smoking. Maybe the root man was Florida's most powerful conjure man, but he was no match for my addiction.

At this point in my life, I had a symbiotic relationship with my mother. From the time I ran away from home at age seventeen she had been trying to rescue me. In my anger and resentment, I pushed her away. She even went and found my father, who I had seen only twice since he left in the taxicab and that had been nearly ten years.

The first time I saw him after that dreadful day, I was around ten years old, my mother had me dress up in my prettiest church dress and without telling me where we were going, we got on a city bus and got off at and some kind of factory. She went into a booth and talked to a man, and then her and I sat down on a bench. It was only then that she told me that my daddy wanted to see me. My daddy? What was she talking about? I was so confused because after my daddy left and didn't come back, I had convinced myself that he really wasn't my father. I had rationalized in my tiny, underdeveloped brain, that if he was my father he would come back. Simple, end of the story. I began to believe in my mind that my brother's father was also my father. I had called him Daddy my entire life because that is what my brothers called him. He was always nice to me, I had his last name, and he never denied being my father.

So, when my mother said, "your daddy wants to see you," that's who I thought we were there to see. I was shocked when I saw my actual father come outside with a big wide grin. I was so traumatized and confused. He acted so happy to see me and I just stood there frozen in what I now know was a trauma response. My mother ordered me to give him a hug. I felt so betrayed by her, but this was a constant

Look For The Purple

response to her. I'm sure I learned before I could talk that she was not a safe place and that I couldn't trust her.

She stood and talked to my father for what felt like an eternity, but it was probably only a couple of minutes. I was sweating profusely and itching from the shame-bumps that were all over my body. My father pulled out a wad of money and gave her a stack of bills. I don't remember saying bye to him, I felt like a zombie, and was relieved when we got back on the bus and headed home. After we got off the bus we stopped at a diner and my mother bought us both cheeseburgers, fries, and a strawberry milkshake and we sat at one of the outdoor tables to eat our food. It was very memorable because number one, I never went anywhere with my mother alone, there were always other siblings around and number two, we never ate out – never. I was so happy that day sitting at an outside table with my mother eating burgers and fries while drinking a strawberry shake. Ironically, that diner is still there although it has changed names several times, the picnic benches are still in the parking lot. After all these years I still feel a tug of nostalgia if I happen to pass there and look at that bench where we sat, but most times I don't bother looking and I have never eaten there since that day. That day, my mother was being nice to me, and I was hopeful that I would start seeing my dad again.

Another eight years would pass before I saw him again. My mother suddenly knew how to find him after I ran away with Mr. Evil. All those years, he was never mentioned, and I had willed myself to forget him. Suddenly, I ran away and become a wild child and he now wants to be my father? Nope, too late, did not need him. In my mind my father was dead. My legal father, my mother's husband, and the man whose name is on my birth certificate died a year after my mom took me to see my biological father. Although, he and my mother had not been together since I was born, he was the man I called Daddy because that is what my brothers called him, and he never said or acted otherwise. My name was on his obituary as one of his children and I resigned myself to the fact that my father was dead, and I blocked out all thoughts of my real father. For years I would just tell anyone that asked about my father that he was dead. That felt better than the truth, which was I had no idea where he was. I was so angry and resentful

131

towards both my mother and father that I spurned their attempts years later when they were trying to make amends.

But whenever I got in trouble, getting arrested or whatever, my mother was right there. And although I shunned her attempts, I knew I could count on her, and she was always the first person I called whenever anything went wrong. One night I ended up in the emergency room of the hospital where my mother worked after another failed suicide attempt, this time I tried to overdose on drugs. It was bizarre because I was home alone, and I still do not know how I made it to the hospital. I woke up with a police officer and my mother standing next to my bed. The police officer asked me where I got the drugs that almost took my life. I told him from a random person in a parking lot, and he left. My mother stood looking at me for a few minutes in silence, and I could tell that she had been crying. I will never forget her exact words. She spoke in a very loving and comforting voice and said "Charlene, you are not a bad person that needs to be good, you are a sick person that needs help to get well." Something clicked for me in her words and in that moment I surrendered.

One of my older brothers had recently stopped using drugs and alcohol and was going to 12 Step meetings. He was the first person I knew that was an addict like me that stopped using. I was amazed by his recovery and thought if it worked for him that I might just have a chance at it working for me. Through my tears of sorrow and regret I begged my mother to help me. She promised me she would help, and she kept her word. She was patient and loving, a mother I had never known, but she had changed. She found a detox program for me and took me there. She went shopping and bought me a bunch of toiletries, socks, and pajamas. While I was in detox, she found a long-term residential treatment program in Orlando, and she took me there after I left detox.

This facility was co-ed with male and female clients as well as adolescent boys, all on the same property. It was a recipe for disaster. I fell for the first man to express a feeling in group because in my world this was a strange and novel thing – a man sharing honest feelings. I was hooked and it did not matter at all that I was recently married.

My husband was in a work release program after serving a couple of years in prison. We were together for a few years before he went to prison, and I stood by him. That meant I visited, wrote letters, and put money on his books, but I was in full fledge relationships with other men. I was constantly in some dysfunctional relationship triangle drama with at least two men. At this point, there were two men asking for my hand in marriage; the drug dealer I was with for a few years that was feeding me drugs, or the man in prison that was promising me a better life away from drugs. I chose the inmate, but I didn't break up with the drug dealer until the morning of my wedding. There was also the old man I was manipulating for money, but decided to keep my marriage a secret from him so the money wouldn't stop flowing. The old man was sort of like a sugar daddy, except I never had sex with him. He was impotent and that was just fine with me. My life was a mess and unmanageable in every area. I couldn't see any PURPLE and I was operating out of a seriously flawed belief system that was attached to my trauma – old and new.

My wedding day was a joke, and I was too dysregulated to recognize the blatant absurdity of it all. We got married while my husband was on a day furlough from work release. I was in survival mode, not utilizing my cognitive reasoning brain, so we had a ceremony at my mother's house, and I wore his mother's wedding gown. To add to the ridiculousness of it all, he had to check back in at the work release center by 8:00 PM. I dropped him off still wearing my wedding gown and I spent my wedding night alone, getting high, wishing I were dead. By the time he came home from work release I was in a drug rehab program. What a lovely couple we were.

Here I was in drug rehab, smitten by Mr. Feelings, who was also in drug rehab. Males and females were not allowed to fraternize with each other, so we snuck around every chance we got. We ended up in trouble for what we will simply call inappropriate behavior. This program was a therapeutic community, and all issues went before the entire community of clients and staff. They held a mock hearing where they gave out consequences, or, as they referred to them, learning experiences. In our case, we lost privileges like phone calls and visitations for two weeks and had to write several essays. If I wasn't operating from a primitive brain thought process, I would have taken my consequences and tried to learn from my mistakes. But, at this point in my life, I was incapable of making rational and healthy decisions, and so was he.

Mr. Feelings and I declared our love for each other in front of the entire community. A very wise counselor said, "Okay you all think you are in love and want to be together, then we are going to let you all be together all the time." And that they did. They literally tethered us together by a six-foot rope, where we were tied together from breakfast until after the last meeting of the night. We both had to wear cardboard signs around our neck that read "Ask me what my meaning of love is" and were constantly challenged by staff and clients to describe 'love'. Believe it or not, and by now you should believe it, but this was my first inclination that I really had no idea what love was. I would stammer and stutter when confronted with the question and I became angry because no matter what I said it was shot down.

Mr. Feelings and I were supposed to be tethered for two weeks, but after two days I was begging to become untethered. The learning experience worked. Mr. Feelings had too many feelings and I was tired of his constant whining and talking. I couldn't stand the sight, sound, or smell of him. I was spending more and more time in the ladies' room because we couldn't follow each other into the restroom. I was humiliated but I cried and begged to be set free from him. They ended the learning experience after a few more days of what felt like pure torture to me. But I did learn that I did not know how to feel a connection with a man without romanticizing or sexualizing it. I also realized I had no idea what a healthy loving relationship was. Although the experience was humiliating, these were valuable lessons.

One of the best things that came out of this program was the family sessions. My family, including my father, was extremely supportive of me when I went to treatment. I thought they would reject me in shame, but the exact opposite happened. My mother, my father, and his new wife who I adored attended family sessions. My father was living in Gainesville, Florida about one hundred miles from the rehab, but they came regularly. Even some of my siblings participated in these sessions and my healing process began.

I completed this program within a few months, although I was supposed to be there for six months. My husband was home from work release, and I convinced the community I was ready to graduate so that I could go home and start being a wife. I memorized most of the literature, I talked a good game, and after a couple of months, I was practically running the groups. This is when I first thought I should become a counselor or social worker because I seemed very good at telling others how to fix their problems. I had every intention of staying clean after I left the program and immediately enrolled in the after-care outpatient program. Within days of being home I realized that my husband, fresh out of work release, was using and selling drugs. We got into a huge fight about him endangering my recovery and to really show him what a bad example he was, I started using drugs again. Another fine example of, I'll show you how much you hurt me by hurting myself more.

There was only about two months between my relapse and me ending up in Boston and those few months were a blur. I tried crack for the first time after I got out of treatment. Prior to that we were freebasing cocaine by chemically reducing it to its purest form and smoking it. Crack was another animal; it was not pure cocaine, and it was mixed with often unknown chemicals. I smoked crack for less than two months, and I can tell you firsthand that it is the drug of the devil. I started to have audio and visual hallucinations along with extreme paranoia. If I thought I hated getting high, I really hated crack.

Crack ushered in the end of our communities as we knew them, destroyed families, and overwhelmed the child welfare and the criminal justice systems. Crack mostly affected the Black communities and drug addiction was criminalized. The Regan administration declared the "war on drugs" but it could have been more aptly named the "war on the Black communities." The prisons in this country were bursting at the seams with Black bodies, most of whom were not violent criminals but in desperate need of treatment. But addiction did not become widely viewed as an illness and addicts stopped being viewed as criminals until the opioid crisis erupted and most of its victims where White and lived in the suburbs.

After being in drug rehab I now had knowledge and information that I did not have before treatment. Information on addiction and recovery changes the game for an addict. I went from being a victim of my addiction, thinking I was possessed, and not knowing that recovery was possible, to understanding addiction and knowing that recovery was possible. I was no longer a victim, but I was a volunteer for the madness. When I first started using drugs again, I thought I could use the information I learned in treatment to control my drug use and not let it get out of control. There is a saying in the 12 Step program, "one is too many and a thousand is never enough". After I used that one time, I couldn't use enough drugs to drown out the information that now floated around in my head. I began to obsess about suicide, and I tried a couple of times. I was so angry that I couldn't kill myself and the only option I had was to try treatment again. I went to my mother and with her help we called all over Florida and then Georgia, other random states until we found a program in Boston that would accept me.

By the time I entered Women Incorporated I was defeated and deflated, yet even with that I knew there was a divine force working in my life the day I sat at that hodgepodge of tables. Yet, there was still part of me that wanted to get up from that table and run. But run where, back home? I came to this program in Boston to get away from that, but I was filled with fear and trepidation. This place was scary, and I was doubting my ability to be successful in such a hardcore place.

Just as I was thinking that maybe my chances would be better at home the Program Director, Diane, entered the room and sucked the air out with her powerful presence. I could tell by the other women reactions, that this woman was in charge. All chatter ceased and the women seemed to sit up a little straighter. Dianne sat at the head of the table in one of the few chairs with arms as though she was sitting on a throne. Wearing a stylish tweed blazer and silk blouse, her manicured hands were covered with rings on practically every finger, and she held a lit cigarette with at least two inches of ashes clinging on to it. After what felt like hours of thick smoky silence, which was only a few seconds, she turned and looked directly at me with such confidence and power it felt like she was looking through me. "So, what is your wildest dream?' she asked.

My wildest dream? The question rendered me speechless as I glanced at the poster on the wall that asked the same question. I had looked at the poster dozens of times since sitting at the table, but it now provided a focal point so I could avoid looking directly at Diane. I felt everyone in the room become hyper focused on me. I felt a mild panic thinking this must be a trick question and I felt terrified that I was going to be humiliated no matter what I said. I felt so much shame about my uncertainty that I wished I could disappear into thin air. My wildest dream? At that point all I wanted was to go to bed at night and wake up in the morning feeling like a human being in control of my life. I just wanted out of the madness that was my addiction. I wanted to feel normal, whatever that was. I wanted to be able to get up and go to work and come home and make dinner. I wanted to spend time with my family and friends without lying, sneaking around, and being consumed by shame. But all I could manage to say was, "I want to stop using drugs". Diane sort of half smiled, blew a puff of smoke in my direction, and said "Okay, we can handle that." I exhaled with a sigh of relief and my anxiety was replaced by a glimmer of hope that maybe they could handle it, that there might be hope for me after all.

When I entered the program, I was told it would last approximately six months and I had calculated that I would be back home in Florida by Valentine's Day (not that I had a sweetheart). I did not have any idea to where my husband was at this point. We had started smoking crack together and it was horrible. By the time I left for treatment in Boston, I hadn't seen him for a couple of days, and it would be a couple of weeks before he even realized I was gone. Little did I know that I would be in the program for fourteen months and it would be nearly ten years before I decided to return home to Florida to live. While in treatment, I would spend most of my waking hours for the next fourteen months sitting around that mishmash compilation of tables and that poster, "Beyond Your Wildest Dreams" became the backdrop of my treatment. A daily promise of sort if I did not pick up the dope.

The program was broken down by phases with Phase 1 being the most intensive component. Everything we did was considered therapeutic and part of the treatment. Our entire day was extremely structured from the time we woke up until the time we were allowed to go to bed, it was humbling and exhausting. Phase 1 typically lasted about two months, at which time we would do a presentation where we petitioned our peers and staff to move to the next phase. I was very excited when my two months were over. I wanted to move to Phase 2 where I would be allowed to get a job and be out the program during the day. I petitioned and was turned down. Staff felt I was not ready to move from Phase 1 to Phase 2.

I petitioned for phase 2 several times and each time I was denied by my peers and the staff. They said I was only spewing information and that I had not internalized any of it. They kept telling me to get real or die. Staff said "You are not ready. If we let you phase up, you will be shooting dope in a heartbeat. We love you and we don't want you to die." That's how it was at Women, Inc., they were hardcore, but we knew that staff cared and wanted the best for us. They constantly stressed that it was not about getting high or staying clean, but it was about life or death. Reframing it as life or death created a sense of urgency and drove home the seriousness of the choice.

Finally, after six months my petition was accepted, and I was able to move to Phase 2. I had spent more time in Phase 1 than anyone else in the history of the program. In phase two of the program, we got a job and saved our money until it was time to leave. Treatment continued during the working phase and in some ways it got harder. I got a good job at Boston Legal Services as a legal secretary. I would get up in the morning and go to work all day like a normal person. I would go out for lunch and relish eating a meal alone or take walks in Boston Commons on my lunch break. But at the end of my workday, I returned to the program with all the drama of a house full of twenty-plus women and children living together. There were groups every night after dinner along with endless essays and we were not allowed to go to bed before 10:00 PM. Overall, this was the hardest and yet the best thing I ever did for myself in my life, hands down. Nothing I have done since can compare to the exponential transformation that happened at Women, Inc. Nearly forty-years later I still give this experience the credit for creating the woman I am.

The treatment model was an old school therapeutic community, often referred to as TC. This model of treatment has been modified because it is no longer an acceptable model of treatment because it was deemed to be abusive, degrading, and retraumatizing. But for decades this was the model. TCs were originally designed for long term heroin addicts. It was thought that heroin addicts had numbed emotions, even after they stop using the drugs, and therefore a highly confrontational and stressful environment was necessary to break them down. It was similar to what happened in the military during basic training. Designed to break you down and expose your weaknesses under stress and duress. This intentional stress was created by using humiliation, bizarre Learning Experiences (LEs) such as forcing clients to carry a large suitcase everywhere to remind them of their emotional baggage; and hundreds of random rules that were impossible to remember or follow. (In my first rehab in Florida, everyone had to say "I'm aware" whenever we stepped out a door or that was grounds for an LE). At Women, Inc. we had to line up at the office door every night, wait for staff to look up and acknowledge us and one by one ask for permission to go upstairs to bed. Janice and all the other women had been right on my first day, this program was hard. A lot of women came and left – some after only one day. Others would stay through Phase 1 and as soon as they were allowed out to get a job, they never came back. Within days we would see some of these women on the streets. They were getting high – they had chosen death. Every day I made the decision to stay, to return home after work, to humble myself by asking for permission to go to bed every night, I was choosing life.

Not only did staff aggressively confront you, but so could your peers and we were not allowed to say anything during these confrontations, and it did not matter if they were warranted. I was confronted a lot in those first six months. I would be sharing at the group table, and get interrupted by a command "Shut up, you are full of [crap]. You need to take off the rose-tinted glasses and get real. The dope almost killed you out there and now you want to sit her and sugar coat it by telling war stories?" War stories is what they called it when we sat around

fondly remembering times in our addiction. "Get real or shut the ___
up." My entire life I was told that I talked too much, and I did. I often
talked because I was uncomfortable in the silence. I would spin wildly
exaggerated tales that I thought made me look good. It had worked at
the first rehab, they were not having it at Women, Inc.

Once Diane was confronting me about my negative attitude because
I had been whining and complaining about being miserable and how
much I missed my family, when she suddenly said "Go upstairs and
pack your bags. I will buy you an airplane ticket back to Florida and I
will personally call your mother and tell her that her dope fiend daughter
is on her way home." I was shocked as were the other women sitting at
the table. No one ever got kicked out over whining and complaining,
and I did not feel that I deserved to get kicked out, so her words sent
electrical currents through my body. As I was processing what she was
saying, I suddenly realized that if I left, I would die, and I did not want
to die, I wanted to live. I knew there was hope for me. I said this to
Diane, and she simply responded "Good, I'm glad you finally realized
it, and now your recovery can begin."

We sat around that hodge-podge table from 7:00 AM until 10:00
p.m. every day. Everything happened there. Breakfast, lunch, dinner,
groups, feelings process, psychoeducation, house meetings, and
visitations. On the weekends when we finally got a break from the
seriousness of it all, we sat at the table and played cards and other
games, braided each other's hair, and chained smoke cigarettes.
The first floor of this house had been converted into a daycare. The
children that lived with us at Women, Inc. attended there if they were
not school age. Although, I was initially annoyed at the thought of
being in a rehab with children, I came to love the children that lived
with us. And those of us that did not have kids pitched in and helped
the moms care for them. We were like a big family, and they were my
sisters.

The daycare was not exclusively for the client's children, but kids
from all over Boston attended as well. One of my favorite assignments
was being a monitor on the daycare van as it drove around to pick
up children in the surrounding neighborhoods. My only job was to
help the children get buckled in their seats, but because I was not

from Boston it was exciting to get out of the program and see the neighborhoods. The van driver was a nice older man. He was kind, fatherly and I felt safe with him. I did not even mind waking up at 4:30 to be on the van and ready to roll by 5:15AM.

There were two main questions that we were constantly challenged to answer. What have you lost because of the dope? What are you willing to give up for recovery? On any given day, the answer to these questions determined if you planned to live or die. Our peers judged the seriousness and commitment to treatment by the answers. We confronted each other and challenged each other to get real and go deeper. It was the epitome of tough love. We would spend hours processing a woman if she was thinking about getting high, or if she wanted to go back to something in her old life (usually a toxic relationship). "Play the tape all the way through," we would say. Constantly challenging each other by asking "and then what?', forced us to go deeper and deeper. As my response to these questions went deeper and deeper as time went by and I became more committed to recovery so did my response to "What is your wildest dream?" They didn't have the brain science that we have now, but we were rewiring our brains, and we did not even know it. Also, by asking each other to answer the question, "and then what," forced us to engage our prefrontal cortex in cognitive reasoning skills. This often assuaged the old or mid brain that was responding to an emotion or primitive response to fear. For all its faults, these tactics worked.

In the behavioral health arena, unresolved issues are often referred to as baggage. Entering a residential drug rehab, you are expected to be carrying baggage. However, there are varying degrees of baggage. Some people enter residential treatment with designer overnight bags full of issues while others enter with a few beat-up suitcases full of issues. I entered with a moving van full of issues that took months to unpack. One of the issues I needed to deal with was to give up and let go was my husband.

The day I left Florida for drug treatment in Boston, he was out chasing his own demons, and he did not even know I was going back to treatment, until a couple of weeks after I left. We were basically married in name only since we had barely spent a night together since the wedding. But I was deeply attached to being married, or to be honest, the idea of being married. I liked referring to myself as a wife and loved saying *my husband*. It didn't matter if we were not together and had never lived together as husband and wife, except a few nights of madness smoking crack together. But with all my trauma and starvation for love, I called crumbs a feast. Being able to say that I was a wife provided proof to the world that I was lovable and wanted even if it was by a drug dealing, crack smoking thief. Touché.

Another issue I needed to unpack in addition to my husband, was the money man I was using to pay bills and provide me with drug money. This was a very bizarre and self-deprecating arrangement. This man was in his fifties, and I was in my early to mid-twenties. He was White, extremely eccentric and didn't have any sexual drive. He basically paid me for companionship. He thought I was smart, bought me an electric typewriter, and "hired" me to be his secretary and personal assistant. Over the years, I may have typed very few documents, but received money every week. He was a consulting engineer with several patents. He did not have any friends or family and he suffered from undiagnosed mental health issues which included obsessive/compulsive disorder. What made this arrangement so bizarre is that he was a racist with a white supremacist ideology. He would tell me often that he wished that Black people were still slaves so that he could legally own me. I resented him and detested everything about him, but I was an addict. My life was unmanageable, and I became unemployable. There were times that I would stop using and try to clean up my act. During those times I wouldn't speak with him or ask him for money. But as soon as I would start using again, I would call him and ask for money, which he was happy to give so long as I accommodated him – which usually meant getting on a plane and going to whatever city he was in that month go out to dinner with him and listen to his insane rants. From the outside if you saw me driving my brand-new car, living in a beautiful home, and dressed to the nine – one would think I had it made, but I was miserable, suicidal, and couldn't stop getting high.

Not only did he take care of me, but family members as well. My family did not support my drug use, but they benefitted financially from the money man. The healthier I became, I knew I couldn't continue to take money from this man and continue to feed my faulty belief that I was not enough, and that I would never amount to anything, which would lead me right back to using.

Eventually, I made the lifesaving decision to let go of any people, places, or things that wouldn't serve me in my recovery. I decided moving back to Florida right after treatment wouldn't be conducive to my recovery. I had a strong support system for recovery in Boston. I knew Orlando was a mine field and with just one wrong step, and I would be blown to smithereens. I gave it all up–the husband, the house, the car, the money man, and the familiar place I called home.

For simple infractions such as not completing chores or being late to group, we were given LEs that usually consisted of writing twenty to twenty-five page essays. Once while doing my chores, I left a broom out upstairs. Nothing major, I simply forgot and left the broom out. Well, you would have thought I killed someone the way my peers and staff responded. My LE was a forty-page essay on "Why I need to be aware." Forty! I couldn't believe it. And to make it worse, I was not allowed to start my essay until after the nightly meeting at 10:00 PM, and I wouldn't be allowed to go to sleep until it was complete. I was livid and I was ready to leave treatment over this assignment. It felt over the top. Even my peers sympathized with me and thought it was too much for forgetting to put a broom back. I was so angry and felt the staff hated me and was trying to push me out. I was angry and I felt unloved, but the fighter in me - that part of me that had survived my childhood, abusive relationships, and addiction, the part that kept me alive decided *I will show them, I am going to write it and then I am going to tell them all to kiss my ass and leave.*

I started writing and the first ten pages were basically free form writing, in which I complained about the unfairness of this exercise and how much I wanted to leave and just go home to Florida. I wrote about my grandmother and how much I missed her cooking. I even wrote her recipe for bread pudding. That was the saving grace about these written essays, we could vent, and free form write as long as we spent a few pages on the topic the essays were acceptable. I wrote nonstop, every nonsensical thought that came into my mind.

But somewhere around fifteen pages my writing began to shift beyond my surface thoughts, and I started to go deep. This essay was paradigm shifting as I wrote about my insecurities, fears, and doubts. If I had to choose one defining, moment in my treatment that changed everything – it would be this essay. I challenged my assumptions and the beliefs I had accepted my entire life. I was worthy and I deserved to recover. I had spent my life being a victim and blaming others for the abuse and trauma I experienced. I realized I wouldn't survive unless I took full responsibility for my life. I became aware that by blaming my mother, father, brothers, etc. that I had surrendered all my power to them. My childhood was over, long gone, I was twenty-six years old, but I still held them responsible for my joy or the lack thereof. I still wanted the impossible - to turn back the clock and have a different past. This kept me acting out in self-destructive and self-defeating behaviors. It was not about the broom, but it was about awareness. I was now aware, and I made a commitment to myself to take full ownership of my life. Fail or succeed, it was up to me. There was so much power and freedom to reach this awareness.

When I went to the office to turn in my essay, the big clock on the wall informed me it was 3:47 AM. Nearly six hours had passed from the time I started the essay. Staff would later tell me that they knew if I only had twenty pages to write I would filibuster the entire thing and not reach the place they were trying to get me. They were right and today I am grateful for that assignment because it changed the trajectory of my life.

I was now aware of my choices. For the first time in my life, I saw a real possibility for a bright future - beyond my wildest dreams. Dianne would periodically pose the question: what is your wildest dream? My dreams evolved as I evolved. Once my wildest dream was getting a job and an apartment and paying my own bills. I was able to check that off the list the day I left treatment and moved into my own apartment. The next wildest dream was to get a college degree. I got three of those. My dreams kept expanding as I set goals and accomplished them. I couldn't imagine the life I have today. It is beyond my wildest dream's dream. But I got here through retraining my brain, changing my faulty belief system to powerful life affirming beliefs, and taking actions that demonstrated and affirmed my new beliefs. Like a phoenix I rose from the ashes of my own destruction and took my rightful place in the world.

I feel that the butterfly is the most mystical creature on earth. From its genesis as a caterpillar tethered to the earth, crawling about with an insatiable hunger – never satisfied. It eats and eats and eats until it splits and sheds its skin several times over. Finally, when it can no longer eat the caterpillar comes to a complete stop and weaves a cocoon around itself. This period of transformation brings great turmoil as the caterpillar literally eats itself and dissolves into a pupa, finally emerging as a beautiful butterfly that bears little resemblance to its former life as a caterpillar. This is often how I think of my life with my life prior to entering Women, Inc. as the caterpillar, and Women, Inc. was my cocoon as I delved deep inside of myself to recreate myself, to emerge transformed as the butterfly.

When I was involved in the 12 Step program, we would have recovery celebration. The custom at these celebrations is a few people close to you would speak about you and share what they saw as your growth, or how effected their live. At my twenty-year celebration my mother spoke about me. I sat stunned and teary-eyed as she shared what my recovery meant to her and how she was so grateful to have me as a daughter. She read a poem that she had written about me where she compared my life to that of the butterfly metamorphosis. She talked about me crawling around the dark in pain and fear as a caterpillar, and she compared my time at Women, Inc. as the cocoon. Tears were streaming down my face when she got to the last part where she stated I was now flying in light as I was destined—and then she said something that was very deep and meaningful "The butterfly is her answer to why."

We often question our experiences and the challenges that we face, however if we are able to see ourselves as the transformative beings that we are our pain takes on a purpose. Who we are today is the reason we experienced what we did. No, not just our trauma, our fears, doubt, and insecurities. But all that is good about each of us was developed as well. Focusing on the PURPLE allows us to see that clearer.

My favorite word in all languages is Kujichagulia. Kujichagulia is a Swahili term that translates to the principle of self-determination or self-definition. For me, this means I will define myself for myself and I refuse to be defined by others. Where I come from doesn't determine where I am going, who I was shall not determine who I shall be. My experiences are my experiences, they are not me. I can choose to integrate these experiences into who I am, but they are not who I am. I determine who I am – not my experiences, not my past, not my upbringing, not my relationships, not my job, or not who or what other people think I am.

What is your wildest dream? If it is not a little scary you are not dreaming big enough. If you could live your best life what would that look like? Create a vision board pasting visual representation of your dreams on a poster board and place the vision board somewhere you can see it every day. It may feel overwhelming right now, but if you set incremental goals each step will get you closer to your dream.

Create a Wildest Dream Vision Board:

Supplies:
Poster Board
Scissors
Glue
5 – 10 Magazines

Flip through the magazine and cut out pictures that represent you living your best life. Use your personal metaphors and do not overthink the pictures. I always have a picture of a lemon on my vision boards because for me lemons represent good health or butterflies because they represent transformation. If a picture tugs at you but you are not sure how it fits, choose it and it will make more sense later. Upon completion place your vision board in a location where you will see it multiple times daily. Set incremental goals and began to take baby steps towards accomplishing them. Take actions towards your dreams that demonstrate your new beliefs as this will help to train your brain even faster.

Chapter Eight

A Life Lived in Gratitude

Thank you for accompanying me on this journey of healing and transformation, and I am grateful for our individual paths that have met at such a perfect time as this. You now have the tools to live a life beyond your wildest dreams. Changing your limiting beliefs opens the doorway to limitless potential and a life filled with joy. Joy is not to be confused with happiness, as happiness depends on external happenings and circumstances such as getting promoted, celebrations, vacations, or shopping. Whereas joy is an internal state not dependent on outer circumstances. Joy is our connection to what is good and what is true even amid trials and tribulations. Joy happens when we find the glimmers of PURPLE in the midst of the brown.

One of the primary attributes of joy is gratitude. As has been noted throughout this book, we have a natural tendency to focus on the negative, which is why we remember painful and negative events much more readily than positive. Families rarely sit around and speak fondly of the sunsets from family vacations taken years earlier. But they will sit around for decades and tell the stories of the missed flights, lost luggage, and food poisoning. Blame that on millions of years of genetic conditioning.

Gratitude doesn't mean everything is perfect or without challenge. However, gratitude is a shift in perspective, a willingness to see the entire picture not just focus on the brown. Gratitude is the PURPLE. Gratitude is not a spiritual bypass – which is what happens when we do not

> Pain and gratitude are not mutually exclusive, and even in the darkest hours there is always something to be grateful about.

acknowledge or honor the grief, anger, and fear and jump right over into gratitude because it is the spiritual thing to do. Pain and gratitude are not mutually exclusive, and they do co-exist. Yet even in the darkest hours of our greatest pain, there is always something to be grateful about.

A couple of years ago, one year after my mother passed, my youngest brother died suddenly. Five years younger than I, he was my annoying little brother growing up, but as adults we became very close. He was the brother that I could always count on because no matter what, he always showed up. The shock and grief of this tragic loss rocked me to my core. I was stunned by grief, anger, and an overwhelming sense of abandonment. Yet, I still found reasons to be grateful. I was grateful my brother did not suffer. I was grateful for the love and the relationship I shared with him. I was grateful because my brother knew that I loved him, and there was nothing unsaid. I was grateful for the overwhelming support that I received from my community. I was grateful for my family coming together and loving and supporting each other through this tragedy.

My brother had the gift of connections. He was still connected to everyone from our childhood neighborhood. He was the one that stayed connected to distant relatives that lived out of state. He found all our sisters (including my adopted youngest sister) and established relationships with them all. He was a champion for family, connection, and reconciliation. In his death, an especially important family relationship between two close family members that had been estranged nearly twenty years was healed instantly at the side of his death bed. I am extremely grateful for this.

I had a similar experience when my father passed. I was in my late thirties, and it was through his death I finally developed relationships with my siblings on my father's side. As we stood at our father's beside as he transitioned each of us had our own separate relationship with our father, but as we held each other and cried when he took his last breath, we recognized the connection between us and have honored our father's life through our relationship and love for each other. My father's death was incredibly painful, but there was PURPLE in the pain.

148

I previously stated some of the things I was grateful for when my mother passed. My gratitude doesn't negate my grief, and my grief doesn't negate my gratitude. I am far from being a Patty Pollyanna brimming

My gratitude doesn't negate my grief, and my grief doesn't negate my gratitude.

with unrealistic optimism. I feel fear, anxiety, sadness, and grief – but my default setting is gratitude.

While writing this chapter the world was nine months into the COVID-19 pandemic and there was no sign of it ending. People were dying by the hundreds of thousands and millions became suddenly unemployed with no income, while entire industries came to a screeching halt. Many small businesses were forced to close their doors and hang up their life-long dreams. Antiquated unemployment systems were inadequate to process the millions of claims – leaving millions without any recourse or income.

Schools were closed and then opened and then closed again. Millions of children that relied on school for a healthy meal were now suffering from hunger and food insecurities. Parents were frustrated and confused as they were forced into the position of homeschooling their children, while grappling with the enormous decision to work and risk their family's health or stay home and risk their family's livelihood. Domestic violence, child abuse, and sexual assaults were all increasing while the social services to assist in these matters were decreasing. In the absence of clear federal leadership or guidelines the states and municipalities were scrambling to try to address and contain the virus. Family members were unable to gather to support each other, or to properly grieve or have traditional funeral services for their loss loved ones.

There was racial tension, civil unrest, and protests throughout the world. There were daily images of people that look like me and my family being murdered in the streets with blatant disregard for human life. We watched excessive violence in horror: a woman shot six time while sleeping in her bed, an unarmed man shot seven times in the back, a knee on a man's neck for 8 minutes and 46 seconds while he begged for his mother until he stopped breathing, a man having a mental health crisis was shot 14 times in front of his mother and children. It was happening on such a consistent basis it was hard to process.

There was rioting and looting in cities all over the country. Whether to wear a mask or not to wear a mask became a political statement, along with save the economy vs. public health. A group of militants attempted to kidnap the governor of Michigan because they did not agree with her mandate on masks in her state. And on January 6, 2021, we watched in horror the unprecedented domestic terrorist attack on the nation's capital based on unfounded conspiracy theories of a stolen presidential election. This country was more polarized than it has been since the civil war and people were living in fear that it was headed in that direction again. Amidst it all Chadwick Boseman who played the Black Panther and was hero to millions of children and adults died suddenly. People lost their entire way of being in life and were grief stricken, angry, sad, overwhelmed, and fearful.

Personally, my life was turned upside down. A year prior to the pandemic I took a risk and quit my day job as the Director of Research & Development for an international organization. I lead the development of behavioral health programs and reentry programming for individuals involved in the criminal justice system. I loved the work but found the corporate politics stifling. I resigned and started my own consulting firm creating transformational change in organizations and individuals. My business was going well. I was a road warrior, traveling throughout the country, with workshops scheduled throughout the remainder of the year. All of that came to a screeching halt, overnight. My immune system was compromised by a blood disorder, so I had to isolate and practice distancing during the pandemic. I was disconnected from my family, friends, and my community. I fluctuated between hope and despair, joy, and grief, calm and rage.

Personal and collective anger, fear, and grief were part of this experience but so was gratitude. I was grateful every day for my health and the health of my family and friends. While there were so many elements outside of my control, I was grateful for the autonomy I had in my own life. I became grateful for the daily walks I was able to take, and the daily practices and rituals that are now part of my routine. I was grateful for virtual connections and the flexibility of my clients. I was grateful for my family's weekly Zoom meetings, and I felt more connected to some family members than I did pre-Covid. I was grateful for the time I had to bring "Look for the Purple" from concept to fruition. I was grateful for the healthy foods I now had time to prepare and that I could sit on my patio every morning, sipping a cup of chai tea, and watch the sunrise. I was grateful for the silence, and for the opportunity to slow down, stop doing, and just be.

We have heard that gratitude has positive effects on both our mental and our physical health. But there are also benefits in other areas of our lives such as relationships and finance. The benefits of gratitude have been thoroughly researched and science has determined that gratitude has multiple benefits. The following table identifies some areas and the benefits found from gratitude.

Life Dimension	Benefits of Gratitude
Health/Physical	Stronger immune system, less stress, relaxed nervous system, improved sleep quality, decreased pain, healthier heart, increased energy, and longer life.
Relationships	Deeper connections, more thoughtfulness, more satisfaction, stronger/longer relationships, and greater appreciation for partner.
Personal & Mental Well-being	More optimistic, more forgiving, more resiliency, better memory, more creativity, increased intellectual abilities, and better life satisfaction.
Finances	Promotes generosity, less spending, more contentment, reduced impulse buying, increased savings, abundant mindset, increased social capital.
Business & Career	More productivity, achieved goals, better focus & attention, a more positive attitude, more valuable to employer, and increased career advancement.

Just like the butterfly my mother described me as, the life I have today is in stark contrast to the life I once lived. I have been homeless without a place to sleep, and hungry without food, I have been sick, and the doctors thought I wouldn't get well, I have been barren with an empty womb and a yearning heart. I have been abandoned, betrayed, and rejected; I have been addicted, out of control with an insatiable appetite. I have compromised myself over and over trying to feel loved, and I have accepted unacceptable behavior just to feel accepted.

It is gratitude that allows me to look at my life – the pain, the trauma, the heart ache – all that I have experienced, and feel grateful. I am grateful for my strength and resiliency, and for my compassion and the connection I feel with others. I am grateful for the wisdom I have gained because of my metamorphic journey. I am grateful for the teachers and guides along the way and the seemingly serendipitous encounters that have bolstered and fortified my spirit. I am grateful because my experiences have made me who I am today, leading me to this moment with you through these words, and I wouldn't change a thing about my life experiences that brought me here.

I am grateful for the process of forgiveness that allows me to free myself from the bondage of anger, resentment, and hate. I truly believe that forgiveness is the highest form of gratitude. I cannot say I am grateful for every experience in my life yet harbor anger, bitterness, and resentments towards people and circumstance that made up those experiences. The two simply cannot co-exist and while we may fluctuate between the two, we cannot be in both places at the same time.

Throughout my work as a therapist and a personal development coach, I have found forgiveness to be the most difficult principle for many to embrace. There is often a misconception that forgiveness minimizes or nullifies the trauma and the pain that was experienced. But this is not true. The process of forgiveness brings your pain and trauma to the forefront where it can be acknowledged, honored, and healed. It doesn't minimize or nullify your experiences and the two are not mutually exclusive.

There are different schools of thoughts on the necessity for forgiveness for childhood abuse survivors. Some think it places too much of a burden on the survivor, and others feel you cannot truly heal unless you forgive. I have flipped flopped on both sides of the debate, and I now stand somewhere in the middle.

My approach to therapy and personal development is person-centered and is based on the specific needs of the individual rather than a cookie cutter, one size fits all. I think this should apply to whether to forgive or not to forgive. If feeling you are required to forgive a childhood abuser or someone that caused you severe emotional trauma prevents you from engaging in the healing process, forget about forgiveness, and focus on transforming your pain. If and when you are ready to forgive you will. That is why forgiveness is often the last step in the healing process. Forgiveness is a process, and it could take twenty years down the road before you are ready, and that is okay. Viola Davis, in her Memoir "Finding Me," stated very poignantly "Forgiveness is giving up all hope of a different past."

Personally, in my life, letting go of the hope of a different past was the key that unlocked the door to the very real present filled with PURPLE - pure, unconditional, real & perfect love everywhere. It did not happen overnight, and it took me decades to truly forgive some of the people that abused me. There were breadcrumbs along the way, little snippets of information that guided me to my truth. Yes, there were spiritual awakenings and paradigm shifts, but it was those little nuggets of information that combined within my psyche to form a greater understanding. This discussion on forgiveness is just that... little nuggets – some information will stick, and other information won't. That is okay because it is true that when the student is ready, the teacher will appear.

Forgiveness has more to do with the relationship with self rather than the person who caused harm. Forgiveness doesn't change the past, but it can change your future. Bitterness, anger, hatred, and resentments do more harm to the person carrying it than they do to the person that is the object of the negative energy. The energy stays within the holder's energy field and affects the vessel in which it is stored, rather than the object on which it is poured. It is the same as drinking poison hoping someone else dies. Most of the people that harmed us (especially in our childhood) will never say they are sorry, they will never ask our forgiveness, and many will never admit

> Forgiveness doesn't change the past, but it can change your future.

that they caused harm. Basing our happiness on what someone else "should" do is a premeditated resentment. Carrying the weight and burden of unforgiveness doesn't change that. Forgiveness is letting go of the weight and the attachment to the perpetrator. I used the term attachment here because anger is a powerful emotion that creates a strong emotional attachment to the recipient of our anger. We do not get angry over things or people that we are not attached to. Rather than minimizing your experiences, forgiveness provides you with an opportunity to prioritize your transformation, rather than your past. Even if you are not ready to forgive, become willing to let go of the illusion of control that anger provides.

Because of the adverse experiences in my childhood, I harbored resentments against my mother for decades. I blamed her and others for every bad decision, every failure, and all my irresponsible behavior. I did experience verbal, mental, physical, and sexual abuse, as well as rejection and abandonment. But I used these experiences to justify my victimhood and my anger towards those that caused me pain. My victimhood trapped me in a viscous cycle of pain, rage, and regret. As a victim – I did not need to change – only those that had hurt me needed to change. The problem with this posture is I was powerless over forcing others to change which further perpetuated my victimhood until I realized I do have the power to change myself. What a paradigm shifting realization. It was when I was able to take responsibility for my life and change the things that I could that my life began to change.

However, this was a process and I spent decades nursing and fine tuning those resentments and it took a lot longer to heal the relationship with my mother. Healing the relationship with my father was not as challenging. He was the absent parent, and I did not have file cabinets stored in my memory bank filled with his transgressions like the ones that I kept against my mother. My father was always kind to me when he was around. He never yelled at me, hit me, or called me names. Ironically, because he was so kind to me, and I felt special to him – when he did disappear it broke my heart and I was extremely damaged by his absence. Because he abandoned me duringmy childhood, it added to my sense of not being good enough, smart enough, or pretty enough for my daddy to care about me. It fueled the sense of not being lovable or worthy. A good father will teach his little girl what it feels like to be loved, protected and taken care of by a man. Because of my father's absence, I did not understand what the love of a man was supposed to look like or feel like. I was attracted to men like my father in the sense that they were incapable of showing up for me and they were not emotionally available. Of course, initially I did not see the unavailability but saw other characteristics of my father such as their charisma, the stylish way they dressed, they were funny, witty – the proverbial life of the party, and of course they had a way with the women.

While I was in treatment at Women, Inc. in Boston, my father came from Florida to visit me. During his visit he apologized for not being there for me as child, and he told me he wanted to take responsibility for the role his absence played in me being in a drug treatment program Sitting across the table from my father my heart melted. Here he was saying all the things I needed to hear and although it was too late for a different past, I became hopeful for a different future with my father in it. My father's personality and charisma made him easy to love. I am grateful because I would have only about ten years to develop a relationship with my father.

When my father told me he had been diagnosed with cancer, it was my desire to have a relationship with him that fueled my decision to move back home to Florida. He died when my son was five years old before he was able to form lasting memories of his granddaddy. But, in the short time, he had my father was an amazing grandfather and my son loved him. As an adult my son looks so much like my father, and he has many of his mannerisms – especially charisma. I am grateful that I can see my father living in the smile of my son.

But there was still much unhealed within me around my father when he passed. I had not been able to move into an adult woman in my father's presence. I always felt like a little girl, hanging on his every word. My father was a great storyteller and the time I spent with him I was mesmerized by the stories he told and entertained by his jokes and sense of humor. But I realized after he passed that he did not really know me because I, Ms. Gift for Gab, hardly talked about anything of substance with him. Even as a grown woman my father felt like a giant. I wanted his approval, and I wanted him to like me. I felt the shame of my addiction and all the bad decisions I had made when I was around him. I desperately wanted to please him, and I wanted him to be proud of me. So, although I had inherited my father's big outgoing personality, I shrank and became so small in his presence. My father never got to know the real me because I was afraid to show him the real me. I was still trying to figure out if the real me was lovable and/or worthy.

I continued to do the work on how I related to my father after he passed. I knew that all the intimate relationships I had my entire life were emblematic of the relationship with my father. My father was now gone, and I wouldn't be able to work through my issues with him, but I also knew that my healing had more to do with my own self-concept and sense of self-worth than it had to do with my father.

A few years after my dad died, I got into a relationship with a man where the dynamics were the exact dynamics I had with my father. I practically worshipped this man. He was beautiful, charming, intelligent, and funny. I fell madly in love with him and after only a few dates I practically worshipped him. We had so much in common, and he checked all my boxes on what I wanted in a man, except he was emotionally unavailable. And unlike in the past where it would take months to figure out that my new love interest was emotionally unavailable, it became apparent with him within a few weeks. But because I was so into him, I ignored the glaring warning signs. He really seemed to be into me, he was kind, generous, and caring. But often after we had a particularly intimate time together where he would profess his love for me, he would ghost me. My Mr. Right wouldn't answer or return calls for days at a time or as time passed in our relationship, the longer the ghosting periods became. And very similar to the way I was with my father, I was always happy when he came back around. I accepted this unacceptable behavior from this man for years all in the name of love.

Mr. Right was a natural storyteller, and just like with my dad I would sit at his feet (at least proverbially) in awe. I shrank when I was with him and became small, which was very different from how I showed up in the world. He, like my father, was self-centered and did not notice or did not care that I did not share much about my life. Initially, I had the same shame around my past as I did when I was around my father, and I was afraid if he knew about my past, he would reject me.

This off-and-on-again relationship lasted for years. But as I became more and more empowered, I began to heal many of the wounds that I was not able to heal when my father was alive. Several years into this relationship. I had a speaking engagement in Boston, and I invited him to come along. When we arrived at the conference, I was in my element, and I was no longer just his girlfriend, but I became the Charlene he never saw. Because I had lived in Boston, there were so many people at this conference that I had genuine loving relationships with, and I was flooded with love and hugs and people wanting to chat. After I finished speaking, I was met with thunderous applause and people lined up to give me a hug, share a word, or take pictures. I really was not thinking about Mr. Right, but later found him sitting in the lobby literally sulking. I asked him what was wrong, and his response was, "Who are you?" to which I responded, "I thought you would never ask".

We are wounded in relationship, and we can only heal those wounds in relationship. We cannot think or theorize our way into healing. It is often said that we attract the best possible partner to help us heal, and in this case, it was true. I had a lot of information on belief systems, boundaries, and healthy relationships. But I needed the experience of being in a relationship that exposed my issues and my faulty beliefs so that I could heal and transform. This relationship, albeit painful, helped me to heal the issues with my father. While in this relationship my belief system changed - I was lovable and I was enough.

However, the process of forgiving my mother was much more convoluted. From the time I ran away from home at seventeen, my mother constantly tried to make amends and demonstrate her love for me through her support. I truly believed my mother hated me and this belief fueled my anger and resentments. But no matter what trouble I found myself in (and there was a lot) my mother was always there. Arrested and in jail – my mother bailed me out, in the hospital – my mother was by my side. Once I was beaten by Mr. Evil and my face showed the evidence. My aunt saw me and told my mother. My mother put her life on the line by going into places she shouldn't have gone looking for him with a gun. Later she would tell me that she would have shot him if she had found him.

It pains me to say that there were months at a time when my mother did not know if I was dead or alive. I now understand that she worried constantly about me. But because of my beliefs and self-centeredness I was unable to understand this at the time. I interpreted any side look or sigh from her to mean that she hated me, and it would trigger my rage. As I was as a child, I had no qualms with letting her know exactly how I felt, however as an adult I often used the most extremely hurtful words.

After I entered treatment things got better, because I consciously worked on forgiving her, and for a while I thought I had. But I was to learn forgiveness is a process not an event. I lived in Boston and my mother lived in Florida, so it was easy to maintain a loving long-distance relationship. Whenever I went home for a visit, she would cook all my favorite foods and always made me feel special. When I miraculously got pregnant, it was deemed a high-risk pregnancy and I had to be very careful so that my beautiful baby could be born healthy. At six months I was hospitalized for pre-term labor after which I was placed on total bedrest. My mother gave up her life in Florida and came to Boston to help us. What an incredible demonstration of her love for me. But because I had not healed the deep places within me that was still holding on to the pain from my childhood, I was not able to fully accept her love.

My mother cooked and took care of me during this crucial time in my pregnancy. I had a long arduous labor, and my mother was with me through it all. I was so grateful to have her with me. She was in the delivery room when he was born along with my son's father and his mother. Things were okay for a while, and then my son was born. I held him in my arms and felt a love I did not know was possible. I couldn't imagine giving him away, and within a few weeks I was in my mother's face screaming at her. 'How could you give away my sisters? You are evil, and I do not want you around my son.' I demanded she tell me where my baby sister was, as she was the only sister we had not yet reunited with. I had been particularly traumatized because she was my father's child and my only full sibling. It was after my mother gave her up that my father, who had been living with us, left in the taxicab. She did not know because she was adopted, they changed her name, and the records were sealed. That was not an acceptable response. 'Why did you give her up in the first place?' She was unable to respond to my onslaught of questions. I wanted her out of my home and out of my life. My mom returned to Florida, and I swore I would never speak to her again. She was in the delivery room when my son was born and there was an instant bond between them, but I was determined she would never see him again. Smug and arrogant, I was going to make her pay.

But I was consciously in a healing process, and my healing required I change my limiting beliefs and let go of the suffering by holding on to my past. I was responding to my mother from my old brain, that did not recognize the difference between the past and the present. Nothing my mother had done to make amends mattered, because my brain was in the pre-amends past. Over time as I processed and dealt with the grief of losing my sister and my father on the same day, and the grief of not having the mother that came to Boston to take care of me when I was a child, I was able to engage my thinking brain and move into the present.

Within a year of my son's birth, I moved back to Florida and earnestly and carefully resumed the healing process with my mother. I know from my own life that people are capable of deep and radical change. If I got what I deserved for every wrong thing I did I wouldn't be alive. I was a living example of amazing grace and I extended this same grace to my mother. Despite her failings as a mother, she was a loving and caring grandmother. She loved and adored my son, and he loved her. He never had to meet the mother of my childhood and for that I was grateful.

As a life-long student, I researched everything I could find on forgiveness. Based on the research, my work with others, and my own process I have found there are three main ingredients to forgiveness: understanding, compassion, and gratitude.

Understanding: What do I know about my mother? About her childhood, her life that could have created the mother of my childhood. I talked a lot with my mother about her childhood and her life. She seemed relieved to finally have a compassionate witness to her story and she shared freely. My mother's story is not mine to tell but suffice it to say that she experienced significant trauma. After understanding her life experiences, who she was made so much sense, and I finally understood her.

Compassion: As a result of this understanding, my heart filled with compassion for my mother. I was finally able to see her as her own entity not connected to me. Much of the suffering we experience is because of our self-centeredness, and I realized that everything my mother did I made it about me, when it was not about me at all. My mother was battling her own demons and I just happened to enter onto her stage. Yes, her actions affected me, but they were not because of me. Huge difference.

Gratitude: The results were a relationship I could never have imagined with my mother. I literally fell in love with her. My love for her did not nullify or minimize the trauma I experienced as a child. My mother made some bad choices, but she was not undeserving of my love, compassion, and forgiveness. Through forgiving my mother and loving her unconditionally, my heart opened in places I did not know were closed. I felt a capacity for love that extended out into the world – I fell in love with the world.

I am grateful I was able to truly forgive my mother and heal our relationship. After my son grew up and moved away to college, my mom was diagnosed with Alzheimer's and shortly afterwards I became her caregiver. The last few years the roles were totally reversed, and

I became her mother until she passed away. I was able to sit at the bedside of my mother as she transitioned with no regrets, a broken heart, but no regrets. I was grateful I had been able to love her and care for her. I was able to lovingly bathe her, dress her, feed her, polish her nails, braid her hair, read books to her, and play our favorite music for her. All with a love that could only come through grace. The following is the speech I gave at my mom's funeral:

When I think about my mother's life and my relationship with her as a daughter it was not always easy. Because of my inability to see the end from the beginning, I often judge the decisions of others as right or wrong. The older and hopefully wiser I get, I am finding Romans 8:28 which says "All things are working together for the Good" to be true, and most decisions are not right or wrong, they are just hard.

As a young single mother of ten children my mother had a lot of hard decisions to make. I did not agree with a lot of the decisions she made, and I spent far too many years blaming her for everything wrong in my life. As a young woman I put my mother through a lot, but no matter what mess I found myself in my mother was right there.

I thank God for His mercy and His grace in my life and the power of forgiveness that led to reconciliation and restoration of our relationship. Over the past few years when my mother got sick, I assumed the role of advocate, caregiver, and finally I became a mother to my mother. I fell madly in love with my mother in a way I cannot even explain.

But I stand here today, and I confess, I am still blaming her. I blame her for my strength and my perseverance. I blame her for my ability to get up in the morning and do what needs to be done no matter what is going on or how I feel. I blame my mother for my love of books and my appreciation for music. I blame her for my compassion, my intelligence, my sense of humor, and my sense of style. I blame her for my integrity, my work ethic, and I blame her for my ability to see beauty and potential where others only see a mess. I blame her for my heart to help others and most importantly I blame her for my faith in God.

When I look at my family, I can think of a million more reasons to blame her because through her so much greatness has been brought into the world. Nearly half of this packed church is filled with my mother's descendants, and I would like them to please stand. Children, grandchildren, and great grandchildren, I want each of you to know that I blame her for you. I blame her for the healing, the hope, the genius, the creativity, the joy, and the love that you bring and will continue to bring into the world by your presence.

People mean well when they say, "God will not give you more than you can handle". I do not believe this. If God never gave us more than we could handle we wouldn't need Him, and we wouldn't need each other. Losing my dear mother, the love of my life, is more than I can handle. But I have God, my family, my friends, and the faith that I know I will see my mother again. Until then…let your soul fly free Mommy.

By no means am I or my life perfect. Yes, my life has been transformed but I am in a process. Case in point, while writing this book, I shared the meaning of the purple acronym – pure, unconditional, real, & perfect love is everywhere with a friend. His response was to sing the lyrics "what the world needs now, is love sweet love." My old brain hijacked my thinking brain, and, in an instant, I was on the defense. "You are patronizing me and making fun of me, I knew I shouldn't have shared it with you.' But unlike the waffle incident, the look on his face registered with my thinking brain and I was able to calm my old brain down. He was not making fun of me, and I was not in danger. I am a work in progress.

Gratitude, love, and joy are my default settings these days and when I wander off the path, I find my way back. This is the truth of who I am. This is the truth of who you are. And this is my invitation to you to step out of the pain of your limiting beliefs and look around for the PURPLE. It is EVERYWHERE.

www.ingramcontent.com/pod-product-compliance
Lightning Source LLC
Chambersburg PA
CBHW021637120626
46545CB00002B/592